The Culture of Evaluation in Library and Information Services

CHANDOS
INFORMATION PROFESSIONAL SERIES

Series Editor: Ruth Rikowski
(email: Rikowskigr@aol.com)

Chandos' new series of books are aimed at the busy information professional. They have been specially commissioned to provide the reader with an authoritative view of current thinking. They are designed to provide easy-to-read and (most importantly) practical coverage of topics that are of interest to librarians and other information professionals. If you would like a full listing of current and forthcoming titles, please visit our web site **www.chandospublishing.com** or contact Hannah Grace-Williams on email info@chandospublishing.com or telephone number +44 (0) 1865 884447.

New authors: we are always pleased to receive ideas for new titles; if you would like to write a book for Chandos, please contact Dr Glyn Jones on email gjones@chandospublishing.com or telephone number +44 (0) 1865 884447.

Bulk orders: some organisations buy a number of copies of our books. If you are interested in doing this, we would be pleased to discuss a discount. Please contact Hannah Grace-Williams on email info@chandospublishing.com or telephone number +44 (0) 1865 884447.

The Culture of Evaluation in Library and Information Services

JOHN CRAWFORD

WITH ADDITIONAL CONTRIBUTIONS BY
JIM LEAHY,
JAN HOLDEN
AND
SOPHIE GRAHAM

CP

Chandos Publishing
Oxford · England

Chandos Publishing (Oxford) Limited
Chandos House
5 & 6 Steadys Lane
Stanton Harcourt
Oxford OX29 5RL
UK
Tel: +44 (0) 1865 884447 Fax: +44 (0) 1865 884448
Email: info@chandospublishing.com
www.chandospublishing.com

First published in Great Britain in 2006

ISBN:
1 84334 101 8 (paperback)
1 84334 102 6 (hardback)

Typeset by Domex e-Data Pvt. Ltd.
Printed in the UK and USA.

Contents

Acknowledgements

In writing this book I would like to thank the following for information, advice or short pieces of text contributed: Professor Jonathan Bengtson at the John M. Kelly Library at St. Michael's College, Toronto Canada; Mike Heaney at Oxford University Library Services; Sophie Graham at the Medical Information and Information Centre, Pfizer Global Pharmaceuticals; Jan Holden at Norfolk Library & Information Service; Christine Bailey and Jacqueline Dowd at Glasgow University Library; Martha Kyrillidou, LibQUAL+; Toby Bainton at SCONUL; Professor Jim Gallacher, Jim Leahy and Nuala Toman at the Student Evaluation Project, Glasgow Caledonian University; Biddy Fisher at Sheffield Hallam University Learning Centre; David Bundy and Trevor Knight at the London Borough of Sutton; Jonathan Gordon, Manager, Market Research, The Institute of Public Finance; Chris West at Swansea University; Jean Sykes, Clive Wilson and Marysia Henty at the London School of Economics & Political Science; Stephen Town at Cranfield University. Finally thanks to Jemima for providing much needed feline support.

List of tables

About the author

John Crawford is Library Research Officer at Glasgow Caledonian University where he is University Copyright Adviser, editor of the in-house journal of Glasgow Caledonian University's Learning Services division, *Synergy*, and he also leads and manages research projects. He holds an MA by research from the University of Strathclyde and a PhD from Glasgow Caledonian University. He has a longstanding interest in the evaluation of library and information services, having already written one book on the subject. He has also authored some 58 journal articles, conference papers etc. He is a member of the Council of the Chartered Institute of Library and Information Professionals and chairs one of its specialist groups, the Library and Information History Group. He is also an external examiner at Brighton University.

The author may be contacted via the publisher.

Overviewing the history of evaluation in library and information services

The purpose of this chapter is not to offer a detailed historical overview of the topic but to highlight some key issues using a historical perspective. Evaluation of library and information services as a large-scale activity is mainly a product of the late twentieth century, however, important examples of survey and evaluation work survive from before the Second World War, and the phenomenon reappeared in the 1960s once the 'poll culture' had been established. The three examples discussed below show at least some evidence of what would now be called the customer-oriented approach.

The Bodleian Library extension debate

In 1931 the University of Oxford published the results of an extensive study into the Bodleian Library. The growth in both the number of books and users and the development of new areas of study had led to demands for improved reference services and more space for stock and staff. The library and its services had grown piecemeal over a period of three centuries and the report authors felt that the time had come for thorough reorganisation and proper planning for the future. The evidence collected included reports by the boards of faculties and studies, evidence from library staff and representations from individual academics. These included some of the leading scholars of the day. Studies were also undertaken of university libraries elsewhere, although the report authors noted that a university library is naturally affected by the parent institution's teaching methods and Oxford had few comparators in this respect. The report did take into consideration some of the other libraries in Oxford but did not consider the college libraries, presumably because of the jealousy with which the colleges guarded their independence. The report only noted that college libraries seemed to be meeting the needs of undergraduates to an increasing extent and that many had collections of great value – unspecified – for advanced study. A 'considerable demand' was identified for a union catalogue of all Oxford college libraries, an issue not to be addressed until the 1980s. Oxford's computerised union catalogue started in 1987 and the first college joined in 1989. Although the reporters had collected data from a range of stakeholders in a manner we would recognise today, political considerations prevented them from producing a report which would have presented an integrated view of the roles of the Bodleian and the college libraries.

The principal user demand was for more monograph and serial publications on open shelves and rapid, convenient access to a wide range of up-to-date information sources, in other words, demands which are familiar today. The lack of demand for loan facilities would be considered rather more unusual. The report also noted that some of the individual respondents seemed only interested in self-contained collections and in their own subjects, and were not interested in an overall library service, an attitude which even in the age of interdisciplinary studies has still not disappeared and was expressed in the debate leading to the establishment of an integrated library service in 1997.

The nub of the issue, however, was whether the Bodleian should be supplemented by a linked but free-standing building nearby or whether a completely new, purpose-built building should be erected on a large site somewhere else. Although impressed by recent examples of academic library planning in the USA which supported the new site option, the reporters unhesitatingly recommended the adjacent site (Broad Street) option. They offered three reasons: the Broad Street option would be cheaper and if the library moved to a new non-city centre location, 'centrality' would be lost. The third reason, however, was much more compelling. If the Bodleian Library were to be abandoned, it would cease to be a home for 'living research'. 'We make no apology for the appeal to sentiment' wrote the authors. However, more practically, they pointed out that the number of students at Oxford was fairly small and that most users would be advanced researchers as there was no immediate postgraduate research. The reporters anticipated that undergraduate needs would be largely met by the college libraries which had been excluded from their study.

The following extract from Oxford's current strategic plan, 'Vision for 2008', specifically the section on long-term accommodation strategy gives an idea of the consequences of the decision of 1931:

The OULS long-term accommodation strategy is also based on a number of fundamental principles:

(a) The decision, taken in Victorian times and confirmed in 1931, to retain the Bodleian Library in its historic buildings (and so build the New Library close by) with all the consequences of space pressures, fragmented development, service inefficiencies and increased operating costs is effectively irreversible. [In the course of its consideration, during 2001, of the plans for the Libraries Capital Campaign, the University's Planning and Resource Allocation Committee (PRAC) revisited this key issue. Since the construction of a purpose-built unitary 'University Library' incorporating all of the Oxford University Library Services libraries (including the Bodleian) were estimated to cost more than £250 million to build, PRAC agreed that such an option was non-viable.] The effect of this major policy decision – felt mainly, but not uniquely, by the Bodleian – is that, given the growth in library materials, staff numbers and service requirements since the 1930s, the University Library Services libraries are all subject to increasing space pressures which cannot be adequately addressed by solutions based on the availability of adequate alternative accommodation in central Oxford.

The New Library (and other library buildings) are now full and the consequence is that Oxford University Library Services must now outhouse at a rate commensurate with its intake (300,000 items a year) until major new premises are available.

Although adopting methodologies recognisable today, the report was lacking in objectivity and reached important conclusions about the role of the college libraries which had formed no part of the survey.

The Edinburgh public libraries survey (1936)

Ernest A. Savage was one of the leading public librarians of his day and a pioneer of survey and evaluation to facilitate planning especially in demonstrating the need for new branch libraries. His aim was to identify patterns of book borrowing to discover which areas were well or ill-served. He did this by making an analysis of all books on loan on one day in October 1936, rather than just the books issued on that day (Savage, 1937). The data collected were analysed in terms of geographical distribution of readers. Up to this time it had been assumed that a branch's users were contained within a circle, the branch itself forming the centre of the circle. Savage was able to show that this view was too simplistic. The greatest density of borrowing, he found, was always located on the suburban side of the branch, not on the townward side. The geographical boundaries of a branch's membership were affected by factors like canals and railway lines, and notably by cheap, public transport which could greatly extend a branch's membership base. Large, well stocked branches, he found, located half-way between the city centre and the city boundary were the most attractive option for suburban users. The implication, however, that the central library would lose business did not apply as long as the central library was well served by public transport. It would attract users from the whole city to use both its lending and reference facilities. Savage regretted the fact that a network of branches had grown up which ignored modern transport links, were poorly distributed and consequently a poor use of resources. His rather surprising overall conclusion was that the city needed only two libraries, a central library of 250,000 volumes and a large branch, containing 100,000 volumes only about a mile away. Efficient public transport networks would ensure their heavy use, the need to buy multiple copies would be much reduced, overhead costs would be greatly reduced and staff could be used much more effectively. In these two libraries high quality, specialist services could be developed. Although he did not develop the theme, Savage also noted that book borrowing was far heavier in areas provided with good quality, working class housing than in unsanitary, overcrowded housing conditions.

Savage's analysis was radical for its time, partly because it took into account the growth of public transport; however, Savage assumed that this pattern would remain unchanged and his analysis depended heavily on a factor over which he had no control. How would such a model have fared in an age of private transport and large volume car parking?

The Londoner and His Library

The Londoner and His Library (Groombridge, 1964) followed a mass observation survey conducted in 1947 (a technique described in Chapter 3) and a survey conducted in 1959 by the Society of Young Publishers. Partially funded by the Library Association and informed by a consumerist ideology – it is notable for the appearance of the word *satisfaction* – it reported on the views of 1,300 respondents and set out to address some of the difficult issues which progressive librarians had already highlighted. The term *impact* is mentioned in the text in terms of low usage in proportion to registered membership, high turnover of members and a continuing failure to engage with the working class, or what would nowadays be called *social inclusion.* The report found that, although public libraries were held in high regard, most people did not belong to them. Lapsing membership and non-use were highlighted as important issues and among the reasons identified were 'ugly buildings pervaded by an official atmosphere', inappropriate stocks and poor display. The heterogeneous nature of user groups and the lack of awareness of services were also highlighted. A quarter of former users were found to have lapsed because they could not find appropriate books. More flexible opening hours were needed and library staff, Groombridge thought, should become more helpful – like staff in stores. The idea of having staff to guide users to relevant parts of the library was even suggested. The report concentrated mainly on book lending, only briefly reviewing non-print services and commenting adversely on reference departments. The survey instrument paid relatively little attention to non-print services.

Today Groombridge's report makes rather depressing reading because so many of the issues he highlighted are still unresolved, although undoubtedly public libraries present a much more welcoming face to the user than they did in the early 1960s. Also noteworthy is the focus on the lending service. Libraries today are expected to provide audiovisual, information and electronic services as well.

One comment in particular was an important pointer to the future:

> ...those librarians who believe some sociological understanding of the people in their areas to be an essential complement to their professional skills, are surely those likely to advance the service to new levels of public relevance and successful provision. (Groombridge, 1964: 90)

Progress to a new agenda

In the early 1960s Aslib noted that the purpose of the whole library system is to satisfy readers but went on to observe that little attempt appeared to have been made to find out how satisfied readers actually were. Subsequent developments were influenced by outside events. The growth of the consumer movement in the 1970s encouraged consumers of goods and services to view much more critically the quality of services they received and to complain if they were not satisfied. Declining patterns of public expenditure in the mid-1970s indicated the need to maximise resources and defend pre-existing patterns of expenditure. This sometimes required the collection of data. Economic recession also encouraged consumers to spend more carefully and look more critically at the goods they purchased and the services they funded, either directly or indirectly.

These factors informed an increasingly sophisticated approach to performance evaluation within the profession (Blagden and Harrington 1990). Performance assessment concepts were emerging. Monitoring performance began to be seen to be an integral part of good management which needed to be undertaken to convince funders and clients that the service was delivering the benefits that were expected when the investment was made, and as an internal control mechanism to ensure that resources were being used efficiently and effectively. This introduced concepts like *effectiveness* – the degree to which a system achieves its stated objectives and *value* – the degree to which a system contributes to user needs. The idea of usage as the best indicator of value also emerged. Another key idea was the concept of *goodness* to distinguish between how good the library is and how much good it does. Various methodologies like cost-benefit analysis, and unobtrusive testing emerged but, as Blagden and Harrington pointed out, while there was a wide range of credible low-cost approaches to performance evaluation, use of them was not widespread and a significant lack of replication made judgments on their reliability impossible. The focus of library evaluation, the writers thought, should be to show the part that libraries and librarians play in enriching the minds of users. The emphasis of performance measures should be increasingly based on outputs. This signalled a move to user-oriented performance measurement.

Among the key documents this movement was to produce was *Measuring Academic Library Performance* (Van House et al., 1990), a practical survey manual whose general satisfaction survey template proved influential on both sides of the Atlantic and helped to develop widely recognised performance indicators, standardised methods of data collection and reliable data which could be used for comparative purposes. A comparable document in public libraries was *Keys to Success* (King Research Ltd., 1990). This was the first successful manual of performance indicators for public libraries and was published to encourage public librarians to use quantitative methods for setting and assessing performance standards. It listed 21 performance measures and 16 performance indicators with explanations as to how they could be applied. Like *Measuring Academic Library Performance* it was very much a practical manual. The early 1990s was to be a key developmental period.

2

Reasons for and factors in evaluation

Since the early 1990s, a range of factors have been at work, both external and internal to the profession, which have fuelled the drive to an evaluation culture.

Chapter 1 showed that librarians have recognised the importance of identifying and trying to satisfy users' needs as far as possible for many years, while the customer care movement in the 1990s emphasised the importance of a customer-oriented service. The movement originated in retailing but successfully transferred itself to the public sector. The emphasis on customer care expressed itself in customer care statements and charters. The Citizens' Charter led, among other things, to the former Library Association's Model Charter which was produced at government prompting.

All types of library have been influenced by a new world of analysis and assessment. The 'new managerialism' of the 1990s promoted an emphasis on strategic planning, customer service and devolved budgeting in the public services. Strategic planning resulted in the introduction of mission statements and institutional targets, aims and goals, and departments within organisations, such as libraries, developed their own mission statements which could be used as a base for evaluation. The need to identify costs to give the best value for money implies evaluation and led to a shift in thinking. This was notably the case in the USA where, in the 1970s, many academic libraries were regarded as 'bottomless pits' by academic administrators because of the constant demands for more money to keep up with publishing output. The assumption underlying these demands was that collection size and library service quality were the same thing (Hernon and Altman, 1998: 2) something which would not be accepted today.

As budgets declined, so users' expectations changed. Early studies had concentrated mainly on the supply of books, but by the 1990s users expected audiovisual materials, games and CD-ROMs as well as lending and reference services, and with the coming of the People's Network, computers and access to the Internet. How these services were perceived and used added a new dimension of need to evaluation. More recently, librarians have become aware of the concept of competition. Before the audiovisual and electronic information revolutions, libraries had few competitors in the information marketplace. Public libraries today, however, face strong competition from bookshops, whether in the high street or via Internet providers such as Amazon and from the vendors of audiovisual resources like Virgin Megastores. Academic libraries too, are no longer the sole repositories of scholarly information. They participate in a shared, distributed information environment including government, private information providers, scholarly societies, campus departments and IT services. The present century will bring new competitors, technologies and expectations, and librarians will have to recognise these and prepare to confront them if they are to survive in the information marketplace.

Just as services have multiplied, so the understanding of users has changed. User groups are no longer perceived as a homogeneous mass but as heterogeneous groups with different and even conflicting needs which need to be identified and met as far as resources allow. User groups in public libraries are understood to include ethnic minorities, the disabled, the elderly, and children and young people among others. In higher education, categories like part-time students and taught postgraduate students are recognised in addition to the full-time undergraduates who still constitute the highest percentage and at whom, services tend to be targeted, whether fairly or unfairly. A classic example of this is the short loan collection which is founded on the principle that students can always be physically present to use it. This directly discriminates against part-time students, perhaps a working mother with a full-time job who will be lucky to spend 20 minutes a week in the library. These disparate groups are often referred to as 'stakeholders'.

Another factor is the increasing value which is being placed on information. As Booth and Brice (2004: 6) point out, 'For the first time, in modern history at least, the skills of the information worker have become recognized as pivotal to the conduct of practical and useful research'. The more a service is 'valued' the more important it is to find out why this is, whether it is for academic research or, more practically, advocacy for increased resources or public relations purposes.

Evaluation in public libraries in the UK has been informed by the concept of *best value*, which was adopted for all public services in 2000 to replace compulsory competitive tendering. It applies to all local authority services, not just libraries. The key objective is to increase the quality of local services and the efficiency and economy with which they are delivered. It is informed by four principles, the four 'C's:

- challenging the purpose of services;
- comparing performance;

■ consulting the community;

■ competition.

Community consultation involves questionnaires and local focus groups. A local best value performance plan has to be produced each year, reporting on past and current performance and on future priorities and targets for improvement.

In higher education, a steady decline in staff–student ratios has meant that the traditionally close relationship between lecturers and students has all but disappeared, with the result that informal means of communication between students and their teachers have become less effective in securing reliable feedback. Modular forms of course organisation have, whatever their other merits, added to the anonymity of the student experience and a further decline in the opportunities for informal interaction and communication. Ironically, the pressures of external quality assurance for teaching have also reduced the time available for informal face-to-face meetings between staff and students, something which is probably not confined to higher education. These trends have all led to the gradual replacement of the informal by the formal, of which the widespread introduction of student feedback surveys has been a conspicuous part. These and other feedback mechanisms often give an opportunity to comment on the library and other support services. In higher education, as indeed in all other areas, quality assurance has to achieve a balance between accountability and improvement, and it has been suggested that reactions to some aspects of quality assurance have been marked by compliance rather than commitment (Brennan and Williams, 2004: 9–10)

Finally, and somewhat surprisingly, the evaluation of library and information services has become a subject of public interest and debate. This has shown itself in the press coverage of Audit Commission reports on public libraries, and, more recently, the media attention generated by the Coates (2004) report, which was based heavily on one public library service. The reliability and comparative applicability of the data in the report was hotly debated within the profession but it also caused much public interest, even extending to discussions on popular radio programmes. Librarians must be sufficiently knowledgeable about evaluation both to participate in and inform these debates.

These pressures have led to a plethora of agencies both external·to the profession and located within it. While it has been argued in general terms that the performance indicator culture has greatly reduced workplace independence and that trust has been replaced with accountability, it can at least be said that librarians have been active participants in the performance measurement culture and have been active in designing their own performance indicators.

What is being measured?

In order to evaluate a service, it (or a part of it) must be measured in some way – so what forms of measurement are available and what is being measured? A range of options is defined in Poll and te Boekhorst (1996), British Standards Institution (1998), Hernon and Altman (1998) and Davies and Creaser (2005). However, there is still much debate on the interpretation of particular terms and the performance measurement of electronic services, while the development of ideas around value and impact has only served to make the situation more complex. Some key terms are:

- *Performance indicator*: A numerical or verbal expression derived from library statistics or other data used to characterise the performance of a library.

- *Inputs*: Resources that are applied to providing a service and will include financial and other data. These include total expenditure and specific parts of it, such as the bookfund, spending on staff, opening hours, number of reader places and number of workstations.

- *Outputs*: The products and services created by the library. This would include issue statistics, visits made to a service, number of interlibrary loans requested and other, often statistical measures of use. It may also include qualitative data, such as the reliability and accuracy of information provided. Qualitative outcomes are usually more difficult to establish.

- *Outcomes*: The contribution that a service makes to the activities of the user whether they are related to work, learning or leisure. They represent the interaction between user and service. Service penetration (the level of active members of a service) offers an indication of outcomes as does the amount of repeat use of a service.

- *Impacts*: These describe the broader influence that the service has on the community or organisation. Impact can be interpreted as the difference made by the service in the long term.

- *Satisfaction*: The sense of contentment that arises from an actual experience in relation to an expected experience. Expectations are essential here, as the degree to which expectations conform to or deviate from experience is the pivotal determinant of satisfaction.

- *Value*: Value looks at the customer and how the customer approaches the library service. It measures the experience against the cost of the customer in using the library against the cost (time, effort or money) of doing something else. This might include willingness to pay for services.

■ *Quality*: Quality is a much discussed concept (Brockman, 1997: 3–5) and there are many definitions, the simplest of which is 'fitness for purpose' or 'conformance to requirements'. Customer needs are accepted as paramount and quality is defined by the customer. A more formal (British Standards Institution) definition is 'The totality of features and characteristics of a service that bear upon its ability to satisfy stated or implied needs'. In practice, user perceptions of quality are often intangible and difficult to measure, although users are often referring to intangibles when they talk about quality, for example, the friendliness of the staff.

Service and research strategies

As well as the familiar performance issues which inform evaluation, other factors, deriving from recent or current service and research concerns, have crept in to inform the debate. Among these is lifelong learning, an acknowledgment that learning does not stop with the end of full-time education, and that the opportunity to learn expands the quality of life of those who are working, unemployed, retired or planning a career or life change. For such people, the ability to find and evaluate information is important, bringing with it a need to understand and evaluate what is often a complex process, and one not susceptible to the application of crude performance indicators, as these may reflect a repertoire of issues inappropriate to a complex and fluid situation. 'Softer', more qualitative methods are often needed.

Social exclusion is an associated issue, primarily, but not exclusively, viewed as a public library issue and one which refers back to points made in Chapter 1. It focuses on the socially excluded: who they are, what their needs are and where they live. There is a significant overlap between poverty and exclusion. Most people below the poverty line are also socially excluded. Social class also matters. People in Social Class IV and V are much more likely to be out of work, less likely to have qualifications and, even if working, less likely to receive training (Muddiman et al., 2000: 4–8). Both historically and contemporaneously, public libraries have failed to engage with such people and, again, standardised performance indicators are of little use in understanding their needs. As Pateman (2004) has controversially pointed out, public library users tend to be white, middle class, middle-aged and female. Not enough is known about the ethnicity, class, occupation, gender and age of visitors to the library. Public libraries do not engage with the 40 per cent of non-users who are labelled 'hard to reach'. He suggests a good practice checklist which emphasises the role of outreach and making partnerships with other organisations, although more traditional issues, such as flexible opening hours are also mentioned, as is the need for evaluation to identify and build on successes.

Other factors are more located within the profession. Value and impact are essentially outcome measures relating to those things which happen as a result of output measures, such as issue statistics (Brophy, 2002). Value and impact address the questions on what difference the library service makes to the user; what good the library does; and how it changes lives. These measures are the most valuable but also the most difficult to calculate. Impacts may be positive or negative, although librarians in practice tend to focus on the positive ones. Impacts may be what was intended or something different. They may result in changed attitudes or behaviours. They may even influence a product which was an outcome of service use, such as a student essay, piece of research or even home DIY work. There are different levels of impact, the lowest level of which is hostility as a result of disappointment with the service. The user may be dismissive, feeling that the service is not worthwhile. The service may leave the user entirely indifferent. More positively, awareness may be raised even if there is no definite impact or the user may be better informed as a result of contact with the service.

The higher levels of impact are:

- *Improved knowledge*: The user has considered the information obtained and is now more knowledgeable.

- *Changed perception*: The knowledge gained has resulted in a change to the way that the user looks at the subject. Real learning has taken place.

- *Changed world view*: The user has been transformed by the service and constructive learning has taken place which will have long-term effects.

- *Changed action*: The user has acted in a way they would not have done before.

Service providers, however, must be aware that what is achieved may well be very different from what was intended. This will be discussed further in practical examples in Chapter 6.

The ideology of information literacy is one of the most striking information ideologies of the new century and has worldwide implications. There are many definitions, but the one adopted by the Chartered Institute of Library and Information Professionals (*http://www.cilip.org.uk/ professionalguidance/informationliteracy/definition/*) has the advantage of covering all types of service:

Information literacy is knowing when and why you need information, where to find it, and how to evaluate it, use and communicate it in an ethical manner.

This definition implies several skills. We believe that the skills (or competencies) that are required to be information literate require an understanding of:

- A need for information;
- The resources available;
- How to find information;
- The need to evaluate results;
- How to work with or exploit results;
- Ethics and responsibility of use;
- How to communicate or share your findings;
- How to manage your findings.

Information literacy is linked to lifelong learning and social inclusion because it potentially links all types of library, including school, university and public, and encourages the development of skills which can be carried over into the world of work. It has life-changing potential and can even be viewed as a civil right. What distinguishes it from earlier information ideologies is the exercise of discrimination in the analysis of information and the development of new syntheses of understanding, which is not simply repeating information already gathered or even plagiarism. Because of its pervasiveness, information literacy offers new challenges to evaluation. It is necessary to develop new indicators and recognise new sources of information which users consider important. Information about careers and jobs are particularly good examples, as usage evaluation can involve working with careers advisory staff as well as information professionals.

Evidence-based information practice (EBIP) has developed directly from evidence-based practice in medicine and originated in clinical epidemiology. In the National Health Service, evidence-based practice was seen as a way of introducing explicit standards into professional activity by referring to an independent assessment, based on the body of published evidence (Booth and Brice 2004: 2–7). It has been defined as 'an approach to information science that promotes the collection, interpretation and integration of valid, important, important and applicable user-reported, librarian-observed and research-derived evidence'.

It involves five stages:

1. Identification of a problem or question.

2. Finding, as efficiently as possible, the best evidence to answer the question.

3. Appraising the evidence for validity and usefulness.

4. Applying the results to a specific population.

5. Evaluating the outcomes of the intervention.

EBIP is about harnessing existing research in support of a practical decision. Reviewing the literature minimises the chances of overlooking something or trying something which is known not to work and, although based on traditional information seeking skills, it includes supporting day-to-day decision making.

Charters and service level agreements originated in the 1990s and are now common. Charters are more user-oriented and specify what the library will deliver to the user, and in return, indicate what behaviours are expected of the user. Although useful for making it clear what is expected of both service provider and service user, it is important for users to have some involvement in the design of the charter if they are to have any respect for it. The customer care promises made in the charter can be a useful basis on which to plan evaluation. Service level agreements are found mainly in higher education and usually specify what the library will deliver to stakeholders, such as academic staff. However, although the library can specify what it will provide, it is in no position to demand reciprocal standards of service. The library can guarantee that it will process reading lists within a certain number of weeks but it can only request timely submission of lists by academic staff.

To get a complete picture of the quality of library services a combination of measures and techniques are necessary. These include:

- charters, codes of practice, contracts and service standards;
- performance indicators and statistics;
- surveys and qualitative methods;
- unobtrusive testing – mystery shopper approach;
- commitment and involvement of all levels of staff;
- third-party accreditation and awards.

Commonly found measures

There is now a range of indicators common in various types of library including those of relatively recent development because of the development of electronically-based services. These include:

- visits made to a service (both physically and virtually);
- number of items loaned;
- range of stock;

- ease/speed of catalogue consultation;
- requested and reserved items fulfilled;
- documents or photocopies supplied;
- opening hours;
- easy physical access to buildings;
- Internet for public use;
- number of workstations;
- access to electronic information resources in the library, at home and in the workplace;
- staff helpful/knowledgeable;
- environment (comfort, heating ventilation, noise);
- quality of customer care;
- internal signage;
- number of reader places;
- maintenance of equipment (workstations etc.);
- quality of information/reference services;
- access to information about services (leaflets, web pages).

External monitors

The Audit Commission

http://www.audit-commission.gov.uk/

The Audit Commission's aim is to minimise bureaucracy and maximise its impact on the public services it evaluates. These comprise local government, health, criminal justice and housing. The Audit Commission has an important role in promoting the use of performance indicators and was responsible for defining, collecting and publishing the national Audit Commission Performance Indicators (ACPIs). It also runs a helpline on the Best Value Performance Indicators (BVPIs) and provides guidance on the use of performance indicators. There are over 170 BVPIs for local authorities but only a few relate specifically to libraries, although some indicators on cultural services as a whole include libraries. BV 114 deals with the adoption of local cultural strategies including libraries; BV 117 is the number of physical visits to public library premises per 1,000 population; while BV 118 is the percentage of library users who found the book/information they wanted and were satisfied with the outcome. The latter indicator is tested using the PLUS survey instrument which is described in Chapter 4. Libraries are best searched for on the website using a site search which yields over 200 reports on individual local authorities and provides valuable comparative benchmarking data.

The Improvement and Development Agency

http://www.idea.gov.uk/aboutus/

The Improvement and Development Agency is more of an ideas organisation and aims to stimulate and support continual and self-sustaining improvement and development within local government by connecting ideas and expertise both within and beyond local government, by focusing on best practice and forward thinking, by delivering a flexible range of tools and services and by innovating and developing new initiatives. It is a company wholly owned by the Local Government Association. Most of the information on the website relates to the public library in the context of other activities rather than in its own right.

The Quality Assurance Agency

http://www.qaa.ac.uk/

The Quality Assurance Agency is the quality assurance body for higher education in the UK and was founded in 1997. Its mission is to safeguard the public interest in sound standards of higher education qualifications and to encourage continuous improvement in the management of the quality of higher education. One of its major functions is reviewing standards and quality in universities. This principally takes the form of institutional audits which overview university performance as a whole, in addition to academic review at subject level, which looks at specific subject areas.

An example of the first category is the University College London Quality Audit Report completed in August 2000 which contains a short report on the library:

> [para] 58 UCL's Library maintains a number of specialist collections, but focuses principally upon the needs of undergraduates and taught postgraduates. In addition, some departments maintain their own local library facilities and staff and research students also have access to other library facilities, such as the British Library and the London University Library. UCL has a substantial range of digital resources available for both staff and students. While, overall, UCL's library provision was acknowledged by staff and students to be robust, the audit team learnt through discussion and supporting information provided in the base room of instances where concerns had been expressed. It appeared that these concerns had been occasioned largely by increased demand brought about through the expansion in student numbers and as a result of some institutional mergers. In particular, students have

sought expanded and more accessible facilities and enhanced opening periods. Responding to such concerns, UCL has embarked upon a programme of construction and reorganisation. While UCL's Library Services were in a period of change at the time of the visit, from the available evidence it appeared to the team that the Library maintained a constructive dialogue with interested groups, including the UCL Library Committee, faculty library committees, and departmental library committees. In addition, each academic department has a library representative who can further represent departmental views to the appropriate subject librarian and student course evaluations are considered by departmental committees, from which relevant material is passed on to the Director of Library Services. Additionally, the Library directly canvasses student opinion every two years.

This survey reports on familiar problems, such as more accessible facilities and opening hours. The discussion of mechanisms for review and evaluation is of particular interest.

Specific subject areas include reports on subject teaching in individual institutions. A subject review report of March 2001 on the teaching of economics at Manchester University gives an impressive evaluation of library services:

> [para] 38. Library resources are excellent. The John Rylands University Library possesses 30,000 books and 180 periodicals in economics, and current spending levels ensure that material is regularly updated. A large number of journals are available electronically. A short-loan section contains books recommended in reading lists and study packs produced by tutors. Further

assistance to undergraduates is provided by the Lewis Library, which is very well stocked with extra copies of books that are in heavy demand. Students are given an induction to the library by the subject librarian during the first week of their studies. There is effective liaison between the School and the library. Students are content with the opening hours of the main library, and there is ample study space. There is wheelchair access to the main library and a retrieval service on the ground floor for the Lewis Library.

Most of the issues covered are familiar but the specific mention of disabled access points to a widening of performance issues.

Department for Culture, Media and Sport

http://www.culture.gov.uk/libraries_and_communities/default.htm

The libraries and communities area within the Department for Culture, Media and Sport (DCMS) website brings together a wide range of information on the UK public library service. As well as providing current news it includes information about the Advisory Council on Libraries, an expert group on public libraries; the Framework for the Future document, the UK Government's first ever public libraries strategy, launched in 2003; information about the People's Network with further links; and most usefully, Public Library Standards. DCMS looks at the performance of library authorities through the assessment of their position statements, which outline their engagement with the Framework for the Future and their standards regarding public library standards. The standards represent a basket of input and output targets across key areas of library activity.

Information about library position statements can be found at *http://www.libplans.ws/*. This includes local authorities' annual library position statements, guidelines to assist in the preparation of position statements and the standard report questionnaire which all authorities must complete. There is also a frequently asked questions section and a discussion forum. In addition, there is a database of good practice which is searchable by topic. The selection of the topic 'evaluation' draws attention to evaluation work at Durham and Newcastle upon Tyne. The latter includes:

- appointment of staff to evaluate and monitor early years literacy initiatives in libraries;
- evaluation of summer reading schemes;
- corporate customer comment and feedback systems;
- customer focus group and feedback from steering groups;
- partnership with the North-East Museums, Libraries and Archives Council (NEMLAC) around training evaluation;
- issue targets now set for all service points to encourage usage;
- continuing to work in partnership with the Learning City Unit in the evaluation of all lifelong learning provision;
- introduction of pilot projects to enable the evaluation of services, such as Asylum Seeker Bookstart project;
- achieving formal accreditation, for example, the Guidance Accreditation Board Matrix Standards received by the Brinkburn Centre officers at senior management level with stock, reader development and lifelong learning responsibilities.

Finally, the overview appraisals of annual public library plans are available to download.

The Chartered Institute of Public Finance and Accountancy

http://www.cipfa.org.uk/

The Institute also maintains the Public Libraries Benchmarking Club which builds on five years of experience of operation and development, and was relaunched in 2004/05 primarily to address the demands of the DCMS Framework for the Future; the development of action plans, toolkits and practical guidance to improve performance; and the continued dissemination of emerging and established best practice. It is a subscription service which is based around a web-based hub of best practice and information services. This includes an indexed, searchable database of best practice.

Internal monitors

Society of College, National & University Libraries

http://www.sconul.ac.uk/

The Society of College, National & University Libraries (SCONUL) was founded in 1950 and aims to promote the sharing and development of good practice; to influence policy makers and encourage debate; and to raise the profile of higher education and marketing. This includes survey and evaluation work and the preparation of reports, documents and advice to facilitate it. SCONUL maintains an Advisory

Committee on Performance Improvement whose primary responsibility is 'to investigate and propose methods of evaluating and improving the performance and quality of member institutions' libraries'. It produces annual reports, reports on specific issues and maintains the SCONUL template for user satisfaction surveys (discussed in Chapter 4). SCONUL's best known publication is the *Annual Library Statistics* published both on paper and the Internet, which is the main statistical series for university libraries and usually reports on most of the 169 (approximately) institutions which are SCONUL members. Each section concludes with a mean against which the figures for an individual library may be compared. Trend analyses of the statistics are regularly published. These sources are supplemented by *SCONUL Focus* (formerly *Newsletter*) which contains articles on current activities and regularly includes surveys and evaluations.

LISU

http://www.lboro.ac.uk/departments/dils/lisu/index.html

LISU is a research and information centre for library and information services, based at the Department of Information Science at Loughborough University. It collects, analyses, interprets and publishes statistical information for and about the UK library domain. Its publications include biannual price indexes for academic books; readers' guides to fiction and children's authors; and reports of research and special projects. It prepares the SCONUL *Annual Library Statistics* mentioned above. Regular publications include *LISU Annual Library Statistics,* published every autumn, which summarises the current position of libraries of all types in the UK and, where available, trend information is shown for up to ten years. Public library data are derived from the CIPFA datasets (see above) and include some user survey information. Statistics from university and further education college libraries are based on SCONUL statistics.

Children's services are covered in *A Survey of Library Services to Schools and Children in the UK*. This is based on a detailed questionnaire survey and includes tables of individual authority data, with explanatory comments, summaries and per capita indicators, covering children's services in the public library sector and support provided through schools' library services. Less regularly surveys of NHS libraries and secondary school library users are also published.

Centre for Research in Library and Information Management

http://www.cerlim.ac.uk/index.php

The Centre for Research in Library and Information Management was established in 1993 to undertake a wide range of research in the field, including most types of library provision, with a focus on technological and social issues. It is housed within Manchester Metropolitan University and its research work focuses on community cultural development; distributed delivery of library and information services; evaluation projects; accessibility and usability of information; quality management techniques; and performance measurement. It is particularly noted for its work on distributed library services and in evaluating the digital library, and has published studies of the People's Network, non-visual access to the digital library and dimensions in evaluation of Internet search engines.

Advantages and disadvantages of evaluation

A library service which does not practise survey and evaluation occupies a hypothetical point in space. It cannot compare itself with similar institutions to get a picture of comparative service quality and it cannot report to its users on how satisfied they are with the services provided. Information on user satisfaction and service quality cannot be passed on to the parent organisation. It is a measure of how far the evaluation movement has come that it is difficult to imagine such an institution. Apart from some special libraries, most libraries have to participate in some sort of evaluation culture and, thanks to the development of standardised survey instruments, data collection and analysis and interinstitutional comparisons have become a great deal easier. Even when not compulsory, evidence of willing participation in an evaluation culture can add 'brownie points' as the library may appear to be leading other departments. The results of evaluation provide managers with arguments for enhanced resources. Evaluation opens up opportunities for dialogue with users and the very process of evaluation, for example, focus groups, can give users a feeling of involvement in the management of the library they use. This, however, opens up the matter of communicating results to users – an issue in itself which is easily neglected. While standardised survey instruments allow interinstitutional comparisons, they can be overprescriptive and represent a repertoire of performance indicators which do not accurately reflect the work of individual libraries. Fortunately, standardised instruments now usually allow for local variations in practice. Survey and evaluation activity is a practical, not just an academic exercise, and a failure to act on outcomes can undermine faith in the process, although there may be reasons for this, both good and bad. Resources may be lacking to implement needed improvements or the issue may be out of the control of the library. Environmental issues, like heating and ventilation, are notoriously difficult to get action on. It is an error to assume that the results of evaluation will always be welcome; indeed, evidence of needed improvement in particular service areas may not be well received by those providing the service and may result in hostility and antagonism to the process. There is also the possibility that managers may use evidence of disappointing performance to criticise the members of staff concerned, irrespective of whether or not they are at fault. Survey work can also 'fail to deliver' in the sense that it may raise more questions than it answers and only generates the need for further work. Those who participate in survey and evaluation work must be genuinely committed to the process and not simply following a list of externally prescribed practices in which they have no faith. This is why those whose work is being evaluated must always be involved in the process – they may be the best qualified people to participate in framing the research questions to be asked. Finally, evaluation activities must not be too time-consuming as this contributes to hostility to the process. Bill Macnaught (2004) has pointed out that local government in the UK is the most heavily regulated and inspected in the free world and that a great deal of public money is being wasted on setting up audits and inspections. Further datasets are not needed as the performance outcomes of most local authorities can be easily anticipated. What is needed is better performance management.

3

How survey and evaluation work is done

Chapters 1 and 2 offer some background and rationale to the evaluation of library and information services. This chapter looks more at methodologies and explains how survey work is done but does not aim to explain sampling and statistical methods, as such guidance can be found elsewhere (Stephen and Hornby, 1997).

Although the reasons for undertaking survey and evaluation work have been endlessly debated, the essential point is that a library service without a survey and evaluation programme occupies a hypothetical point in space – it has no idea how it compares with similar libraries or, indeed, with other services within the organisation, awareness of which is increasingly required. The immediate answer is not necessarily to dive immediately into the survey pool. In a very real sense this is the last thing to do. It may result in poorly designed survey instruments and unreliable outcomes.

It is important to build on pre-existing work. If you have never done any survey work yourself this will probably mean looking at what other organisations have done, examining their methodologies and comparing their outcomes. It might also mean looking at the work of other departments within your own organisation. They may have developed survey methods which you can also use and identified groups of users who are likely to support qualitative evaluation. They may have identified groups of people in the organisation, such as university lecturers in higher education, who are willing to support survey work because they can see benefits in it for themselves, such as developing awareness of research methods among students. Other service providers may also identify performance issues similar to your own. One of the perennial performance issues in library and information provision is access. This issue is also found in student service provision in higher education, i.e. timeous provision of appropriate services at times convenient to students. Contact with the relevant people may help both to formulate questions and decide what action to take.

Chapter 2 offers some information about sources of information on survey work. If the issue you wish to explore has already been researched somewhere else, you may not need to duplicate the work. However, if you do decide to go ahead with your own study, you have comparative data to use to verify your results and probably a set of methodologies which have been tested. If they have proved reliable you can borrow them (with the originator's permission, of course!) and if they proved to be flawed you can improve on them so the same mistakes are not made twice. You may also have found yourself a benchmarking partner.

While much comparative data will be found within the sector you may also find useful data within related cultures of evaluation, something examined further in Chapter 5.

Quantitative methods

Quantitative methods imply the assembly and analysis of statistical data; in a library and information context this usually means a questionnaire, increasingly a standardised instrument, for collecting general satisfaction data, or perhaps a questionnaire designed to examine a specific issue, such as opening hours, or address the needs of particular categories of user, such as those with some form of disability. There are also other, less widely used, methods. Obviously the structure of the questionnaire and its method of administration will vary depending on the user group being studied.

On the face of it, the quantitative, questionnaire-based method has certain advantages. The questionnaire can report on the views of many thousands of people and give a breadth of data not available to qualitative methods. It adopts a highly structured approach and because it uses statistical methods and produces numerical data its outcomes are perceived to be 'scientific' and therefore objectively correct. If well designed it gives clear-cut answers to the questions asked, and because interested parties can complete it without intervention, it appears to be neutral. Questions based on counts, such as frequency of making a reference enquiry, are easy to collect. The nature of the outcomes and the value of the encounter are less easy to quantify. A questionnaire offering a limited number of answer options of the yes/no or tick box variety (closed questions) can be administered and analysed easily as modern questionnaire administration is increasingly computer administered and almost wholly computer analysed.

The questionnaire, however, has the vices of its virtues. Because it is highly structured, it is also highly inflexible. If a fault is detected during administration, not much can be done about it. It does not penetrate the attitudes which inform the answers. This can only be done by qualitative methods. The questionnaire only answers the questions which have been asked. If important issues have not been addressed then its practical value will be much reduced. Even the most quantitative questionnaire must include at least one free text comments box to allow respondents to air the issues they consider important. It is possible that they will not be those identified by the questionnaire designer. The questionnaire must also be designed to produce action-oriented outcomes. The strategic planning team of the University of Arizona has produced a useful checklist (Corrall, 2002: 27–52):

- If you have conducted customer surveys or collected or collected other customer data over the last 12 months, either formally or informally, summarise the key findings.

- Based on the feedback, what are you doing to meet customers' needs (e.g. projects created, process improvements undertaken)?

- What products and services have been requested that you have not been able to provide (e.g. access to *all* full-text journals online)?

- What would need to change to be able to provide these products or services?

- Looking to the environment beyond the library, list forces that will change the way we serve our customers (e.g. electronic publishing, copyright laws).

While these objectives will help in the design of action-facilitating data questionnaires, it is important to collect data reflecting life experiences. While this can be done by qualitative data collection means, a good deal can be done by collecting at least some personal data. Early examples of survey instruments seem to view the respondent as a very curious creature indeed, one who had no gender, no job, no spouse, no family, and no life commitments, someone who does nothing, in fact, except use a library. Questionnaires have improved somewhat and do at least collect some personal data, such as gender, ethnicity and disability, and in higher education, level of course and mode of attendance. Such data help to build a service around the lives of users and their characteristics and provide flexible services. A student, working 15 hours a week, will want flexible opening and swiftly provided services. As Hull (2001) has objectively demonstrated, women are heavier users of library services than men, being more willing to articulate a need for services and formulate enquiries. A library with a high percentage of women users is going to be more heavily used than one serving mostly men. In identifying human factors in library use, it is often useful to discuss evaluation activities with colleagues in other service areas.

As well as recognising human needs, it is important to present the respondent with a repertoire of recognisable issues with which they can identify. This is particularly relevant to non-traditional library users, such as asylum seekers, new British citizens and university students who come from family backgrounds with no tradition of attending university. This phenomenon was first noted in the USA in the 1960s as a result of racial integration, resulting in new ethnic and social groups being attracted into higher education who came from families with no previous experience of higher education (Boylan 2004). Such people were quite unable to recognise the repertoire of issues presented to them in surveys. This resulted in a major debate about whether quantitative or qualitative methods were most appropriate to studying these new populations, resulting in the conclusion that a combination of both methods was likely to be most successful.

Further quantitative methods are detailed below.

The balanced scorecard

The balanced scorecard is essentially a simplified survey instrument which allows an organisation to focus on a relatively small number of carefully chosen measurements. These measures are aligned with the mission and strategies of the organisation and they provide a quick but comprehensive picture of organisational performance. Scorecards were originally designed for private industry but are increasingly used in the public sector and have now found their way into libraries (Self, 2004). The balanced scorecard examines the organisation from four perspectives: user, finance, internal processes, and learning and the future. Each perspective has one or more strategic objectives or goals associated with it. Four to eight measurements, or metrics, are devised for each category or perspective. Each metric has a specific and unambiguous target or set of targets.

Limiting the number of scorecard metrics forces scorecard designers to decide what is important and to identify the issues which really make a difference. Although dealing with only a limited number of measures, the balanced scorecard approach compels librarians to look at finance, internal processes and the future. Librarians must also decide unequivocally what constitutes success for each measure. Results are easy to interpret and it is also easy to compare year on year performance.

The balanced scorecard has both advantages and disadvantages. It gives a snapshot of organisational health but does not give a three-dimensional picture. It can point out problems but does not reveal the solutions. There is also a tendency to include too many metrics, resulting in a lack of clarity and adding significantly to the workload. However, it clarifies and focuses thinking. It forces library managers to decide which areas are important and what constitutes success in those areas. It shows the need to look beyond traditional customer services and look at collection management issues which also have a role in improving services to customers.

Measurement of in-house use

For librarians under pressure to justify expenditure on resources, measurement of in-house use is an attractive technique as it demonstrates that library usage is much higher than issue and other output statistics suggest. In-house use is traditionally defined as all items of library stock consulted by users in the library but not loaned, which includes reference books, the usage of which is little measured. However, the coming of the electronic library requires some revision of this definition.

Traditional in-house measurement has focused on counting items of library stock after users have finished consulting them (study space use). Such a methodology ignores at-shelf use, which can only be measured by direct observation and has to be measured during a designated survey period, typically four times a day. Wynne and Clarke (2000) found that at-shelf use outnumbers study space use by over five times to one and, indeed, overall in-house use per capita during the period surveyed was more than 30 times that of loans recorded during the same period. Clearly study of in-house usage greatly expands understanding of library use, although methodologies tend to be laborious and time-consuming.

An example from a public library supports and extends this view (Seidler-de Alwis and Fuehles-Ubach, 2004). A study of the Cologne municipal library showed that although loans had remained almost the same since 2000, in-library usage had grown considerably and almost 20 per cent of users were found not to be library members. Apart from books, the main materials used were music CDs, audio books or tapes. In the central library, 20 per cent of visitors accessed the Internet. Traditional indicators were failing to capture about 20 per cent of use.

Qualitative methods

According to Gorman and Clayton:

> Qualitative research is a process of inquiry that draws data from the context in which events occur, in an attempt to describe these occurrences, as a means of determining the process in which events are embedded and the perspectives of those participating in the events, using induction to derive possible explanations based on observed phenomena. (Gorman and Clayton, 2005: 3)

In library and information science, qualitative research is often seen as an addition to quantitative methods as a means of getting an understanding of the attitudes that inform the statistics. Such a method of using a range of methods to verify the accuracy of the data collected by any one technique is known as triangulation and is widely used in social science research.

In practice qualitative methods work in two ways:

- *When something is known about the subject.* Quantitative methods are good at revealing that users are dissatisfied with a service but not so good at saying why. Methodologies based on direct contact with users are likely to be more revealing.

- *When the situation is not fully understood.* Qualitative methods can be used to find out what the problems actually are and, on the basis of this key research, questions can be formulated. This might lead to a quantitative method to collect statistical data.

Qualitative research, like quantitative research, is concerned with context but quantitative research often focuses on a few factors thought to be important or relevant. Both quantitative and qualitative types of research attempt to describe occurrences. The former uses numerical representations to quantify occurrences while the latter uses words to present anecdotal descriptions. The quantitative researcher is looking for patterns in events, so numerical and statistical methods tend to be the most useful. A single event tends to be just one of many being measured and quantified. Conversely, for the qualitative researcher, a single event may be data rich and this richness is best analysed by the descriptive use of language. Whereas qualitative researchers often use the 'bottom up' approach (known as induction) when analysing data, their quantitative counterparts usually rely on deduction. They begin with certain assumptions and then look for data to support or contradict these assumptions. The qualitative researcher is more likely to be interpretative, tending to begin with the evidence and then building theory.

Qualitative research methods have quite specific advantages which enhance and extend the counting culture which has grown up in library and information science (Gorman and Clayton, 2005: 3–17):

- They are attuned to growing complexity in an information environment which requires flexibility and variability in data analysis.

- They facilitate the use of triangulation to enrich research findings.

- They are responsive to the need for libraries to enrich their service imperative.

- They are suited to the non-quantitative background of many information professionals.

- They fit the social nature of libraries.

There are four main methods of qualitative investigation:

- *Observation*: This involves the systematic recording of observable phenomena or behaviour in a natural setting. This is particularly useful for recording unconscious patterns of behaviour which the subjects might not be aware of themselves. It can add a human dimension to statistical counts, such as logins in computer labs which, as a quantitative method, completely fails to record the complex processes of interaction between computers users that is taking place. Computer lab users typically seek the advice of friends or colleagues before approaching helpdesks, which should give food for thought to those responsible for staffing these services.

- *Interviewing*: Interviewing can obtain detailed, in-depth information from subjects who know a great deal about their personal perceptions of events, processes and environments. It is a good way to tease out information about complex situations and, as a one-to-one situation, it gives an opportunity to get to know and understand the subject which is not available with other methods.

- *Group discussions*: To introduce this issue the term 'group discussion' is probably most appropriate. What are often called 'focus groups' is probably the most widely used qualitative method in library and information science, certainly in higher education, and is often used to inform the attitudes lurking behind survey findings, usually in the form of annual general satisfaction surveys. The two methods, taken together, can provide the basis of a robust and continuing programme of evaluation. However, the focus group has quite a precise meaning. They are so-called because the discussions start out broadly and gradually narrow down to the focus of the research.

- *Historical studies which review changing user needs and management response over time*: This method is little used, which is a pity because, as Chapter 1 showed, it can demonstrate the need for flexible decision making and the need to plan for the long term.

Further qualitative methods are detailed below.

Focus groups

Focus groups are worth discussing at some length because they are probably the most widely used qualitative technique in library and information science. Focus groups usually consist of 8–12 people with a moderator or facilitator who focuses the discussion on relevant topics in a non-directive manner. The role of the facilitator is crucial. They must encourage positive discussion without controlling the group. Although the focus group technique is superficially simple, it must be carefully planned to yield useful results. A list of key questions, probably about four, must be prepared to begin the discussion. These should be discussed with appropriate colleagues who have expert advice to offer. Inexperienced facilitators would be well advised to consider 'a trial run' with a group comparable to those who will attend the focus group. Prepared questions should be supplemented by follow-up questions or 'probes' to obtain more information and encourage useful discussion.

Data from the discussion can be tape-recorded as a back-up to notes, in case anything has been missed. A set of notes is also, however, essential, as a tape of what took place in a group discussion might be unclear; in addition, this also saves time, as transcribing notes is time-consuming. Indeed, the tape may well be more useful for capturing how things were said, rather than what was said. Notes should be taken during the discussion to form both a historical record and give the facilitator a grasp of how the discussion is progressing. The notes taken during the discussion can be supplemented by recollection immediately after the discussion. Time in documenting is thus saved and the record will more reliable.

Focus groups have a number of advantages:

- They are relatively quick. They typically take about an hour, two hours at the most and a great deal of data can be collected (but see caveat below).

- Transparency. Participants can see and understand what is going on.

- A sense of participation. Participants feel that involvement in a focus group gives them a role, albeit a minor one, in the decision-making process.

- A form of communication. The focus group is a means of communicating policy issues to users. Participants go away feeling that they know more about the library and its problems and they can tell their friends what they have learned.

- Participants can use their own words and are not constrained by the terminology of a questionnaire.

- Focus groups can raise issues and offer unexpected insights which the facilitator had not anticipated.

- People tend to be less inhibited in focus groups than in individual interviews.

- One participant's remarks can stimulate others and there is a snowball effect as participants comment on each others' views.

- Focus groups are a good way of collecting preliminary information and issues raised can be fed into questionnaire design.

There are, however, some disadvantages:

- The logistics of getting the right people together in the right place at the right time should never be underestimated.

- Dominating personalities. There is always a danger that the discussion will be hijacked by a few dominating individuals. In such cases the facilitator will have to use their skills to draw out the less assertive members of the group.

- Representativeness of the group. Focus groups tend to attract the highly motivated or, at least, those who can be bothered to turn up, and tend to present the views of opinion leaders. While this is welcome, it has to be remembered that such people may not be entirely representative. It is best to select participants representative of the user population as a whole.

- Focus groups are not very good for discussing technical issues, such as the installation of a new computer system, but can be used to collect opinions on the quality of the service the system provides.

- It is inadvisable to overgeneralise from information obtained from focus groups and use it for policy decisions. The focus group technique does not use scientific sampling and it is difficult to quantify the results precisely.

Points to consider in focus group organisation

- It might be worth using facilitators from outside the library. A library facilitator may be perceived as biased in that they may have a vested interest in the outcome.

- Recruiting volunteers may be difficult and it is a good idea to form relationships with units within your institution which have a responsibility for survey and evaluation work.

- Eight to 12 people should be scheduled for each group. It is better to overschedule in case some do not turn up.

- Allow ample time for discussion – up to a maximum of two hours, although about an hour will usually suffice.

- If possible, run three to four groups per population to get a comparative perspective. In addition some groups may not run at all. In analysing results look for comments or trends which are repeated over several sessions.

- Hold sessions in a location near where the target audience is usually based and put up signs. Also notify colleagues who might be asked for directions.

- If possible reward participants for their time even if it is only tea and coffee. Book tokens and photocopying and printing vouchers are widely used options.

There are two variants of the focus group which are sometimes used, the nominal group technique (NGT) and the structured discussion group (also known as a *snowball* or *pyramid* discussion).

Nominal group technique

This technique is occasionally called 'quality brainstorming' because it uses some of the techniques of brainstorming and its members do not need to be homogeneous, unlike a focus group.

There are four steps:

1. Silent, individual generation of ideas in writing.

2. Reporting of ideas which are written up on a board for all participants to see.

3. Discussion to clarify and evaluate the ideas put forward.

4. Individual voting on the relative importance of ideas from which a group ranking can be derived.

The technique can be used as part of preliminary work leading to questionnaire design. The advantage of NGT is that it combines both individual and group participation. Individual participation comes both at the idea generation stage and at the evaluation stage where, if participants are not convinced that an idea is good, they do not have to vote for it. The discussion of ideas and the generation of new ones forms the group approach (Gorman and Clayton, 2005: 151–6).

Structured discussion group

After an introductory discussion, the participants begin by working in small groups to identify and prioritise key themes. The groups then come together and each group is asked to make a point which is then tested with the other groups. Agreement is reached on each point in turn and a record is kept of the discussion, which is verified towards the end of the session. Sessions last between 45 minutes and an hour and a quarter and usually about 14 points emerge.

Interviewing

Interviewing may be viewed as an extension to the meeting method, but by speaking to one person it is possible to probe more deeply into the experiences and reactions of respondents. It gives a friendlier and more personal approach to the data collection process and may appeal to people who are reluctant to participate in group events. It is also a good method of collecting confidential, controversial or personal information which is unlikely to emerge in a group setting. It produces immediate responses to questions and allows respondents to reply to open-ended questions in their own way. It also gives an opportunity to find out why people and organisations behave the way they do. It is particularly appropriate to people who cannot respond satisfactorily to other types of enquiry, for example, children, immigrants and those who have difficulty in hearing or writing. As a method, however, it is open to bias because interpretation is left to the interviewer and the results may be uncritical (Gorman and Clayton, 2005: 126–7).

Interviewing is a skilled, structured activity and must never be allowed to degenerate into a chat. The interviewer must have well developed social skills and must be good at putting people at ease and persuading them to talk. He or she should talk as little as possible and concentrate on listening. It is important to note the issues which are raised and also those which are not raised and perhaps not important to the interviewee.

There are three types of interview:

- *The structured or formal interview*: This is based on a prepared list of questions which is not deviated from. This closely resembles the administration of a questionnaire, except that the interviewer is present to explain and clarify the questions.

- *The semi-structured interview*: The interviewer works from a prepared list of issues. The questions, derived from the issues, are likely to be open-ended to allow the respondent to express themselves.

- *The unstructured interview*: In this case the interview is informal and only the general subject is predetermined. This gives considerable scope to the respondent to express their views but demands considerable skill on the part of the interviewer who must be able to subtly control digressions and tease out issues only partially examined by the respondent.

Interviewing is a skill which takes time to learn and is most needed for conducting unstructured interviews. While notes of interviews are a key source, recordings can also be made. The interviewer should review them with particular care as they may reveal retrospectively that the interviewer has failed to pick up on important points made by the interviewee. Careful listening should help to improve interviewing technique.

Observation and mass observation

Observation and its recently revived older companion, mass observation are relatively little used techniques in libraries; this is a pity, as they have obvious attractions. Observing what people actually do in libraries allows users to be observed in their natural setting and it becomes possible to study people who are unwilling or unlikely to give accurate reports on their own activity. It also enables data to be analysed in stages as understanding of its meaning unfolds. There are two types of observation – structured and unstructured:

- *Structured observation*: This is a predetermined activity where a form is used in which the observer records whether specific activities take place, when and how often. A well designed data collection method will allow space to record unanticipated activity. However, the form must be carefully designed at the outset to allow for this. Because this is essentially a statistical method, it is usually considered to be a quantitative technique.

- *Unstructured observation*: The observer records any behaviour or event which is relevant to the research question being studied. This is a much more open-ended approach and, as is the case with most qualitative research, is especially useful in exploratory research or where a situation is incompletely understood.

The skill of the observer is a key factor and this is particularly relevant to mass observation (see below). Observation is a highly skilled exercise as the observer has to know enough about the situation to understand and interpret what is going on. Even within the general subject area of library and information science, specialist skills might be required, and it may be necessary to enlist the help of colleagues with particular expertise in the research area. For example, an observation study of a newly opened electronic floor (Crawford and Daye, 2000) sought to test the assumption that it would be mainly used for the searching of electronic information databases. A person with excellent IT skills was chosen to carry out the observation and a data collection form was designed, drawing on previous findings (Crawford, 1999) but with space for supplementary observations. The study concluded that the assumptions about the anticipated usage of electronic information sources were largely inaccurate but that the service was heavily used for other purposes.

Observation has disadvantages. People who are aware that they are being observed tend to change their behaviour, at least initially. Observation without consent may be considered an intrusion into privacy. It is not always possible to anticipate a spontaneous event and so be ready to understand and observe it. Not all events lend themselves to observation, such as those which change over time. Observation can be very time-consuming and the subjectivity of the observer can also be a factor. It helps if the observer records their subjective reactions to the events observed.

Mass observation dates back to 1937 when the Mass Observation Archive (MOA) was established to 'study how ordinary British people thought, felt or behaved'. After a busy period during and after the War, the MOA was re-established in 1981 and now employs thousands of observers to contribute observations on a wide variety of topics. Topics are presented to volunteers in the form of 'directives': open-ended, loosely structured, relatively short documents which contain a series of prompts designed to encourage contributors to write at length and in detail. Volunteers are largely self-selecting and are not a scientific sample as they are mainly female, white, middle class and relatively well-off, rather like public library users, in fact. While the MOA method was first used in library research as long ago as 1939, Black and Crann (2002) have been the main exponents of this methodology. They commissioned an MOA study of user behaviour in the public library, designed to reveal what the public library does well, what it does badly and what it means to users and non-users. Volunteer observers were provided with an open-ended set of questions and prompts designed to stimulate the volunteers to write, and were additionally asked to provide some factual data, such as times of and frequency of visits to the library. In this method, the comments and views of the volunteer observers are also analysed, thus the volunteer observers are both researchers and subjects for study themselves. They do not, of course, have any specialist expertise in the subjects they are observing: 231 observers (women outnumbered men almost three to one) contributed 'hundreds of pages of data' which the authors admit is open to a multiplicity of interpretations. Much of the evidence is flatly contradictory. Public libraries are seen as 'popular, welcome and safe places that we love and trust' but they are also viewed as 'declining or stagnating institutions which lack sparkle'. Libraries are viewed as both socially inclusive and preserves of the middle class. One observer described them as 'places run by middle-aged women for middle-aged women' and attitudes to librarians varied from high praise to severe criticism. Clearly the subjectivity and lack of expertise of the observers are important factors and most library managers would not regard this as a method to inform direct decision making, but the apparently directly contradictory views are, in fact, extremely helpful for they show the public library's areas of strength on which to build and weaknesses which must be addressed. Given the key role of women as library users their dominant role as investigators might have merited further comment.

The mass observation method has also been used by McNicol (2004a) to investigate non-use of public libraries. She compared data from the Regular Pastimes directive of 1988 with that obtained by Black and Crann (2002). This drew out such issues as other means of obtaining books, the poor public image of public libraries, difficulties of access due to reduced opening hours, and customer unfriendly procedures. The research concluded realistically that not all non-users can be considered to be potential users and that the marketing and promotion of libraries needs to be improved. The study also showed the comparative, historical method to be useful.

Evidence-based information practice

Evidence-based information practice (EBIP) (Brice and Booth, 2004) is a technique derived from healthcare and is an approach to research, rather than a specific methodology, but it offers a rigorous approach to research which can inform the use of specific methodologies.

EBIP addresses two information pathologies, information overload and the slow dissemination of research findings into routine practice. There are five stages in the process:

1. Identify a problem or question.
2. Find, as efficiently as possible, the best evidence to answer the question.
3. Appraise the evidence for validity and usefulness.
4. Apply the results to a specific population.
5. Evaluate the outcomes of the intervention.

This agenda, especially 2, 3 and 5 is analogous to information literacy. Librarians do not often systematically search their own knowledge database for evidence to support their decision making and these data, once obtained, must be rigorously appraised. As with most other types of research, the most common objection to EBIP is a perceived lack of time, but the alternative is to risk wasting valuable time by persevering with an intervention that the agenda might prove to be ineffective. A brief search of relevant literature will find immediate examples of under-utilised research that highlights ineffective practices that consume large amounts of information professionals' time and resources. Another criticism which may have more validity is the poor quality of currently available evidence, but this highlights the need to critically review the evidence.

Evidence-based practice is a user-oriented process, focusing on questions identified by users or their representatives. Users should be involved in the conduct of the research and in the dissemination of findings; the findings from any research study should be mediated and moderated by the views, preferences and values of the community within which the evidence is to be implemented. This is a technique with direct appeal to the practitioner researcher who should note that the evidence base for information practice is derived not just from library and information science databases but also databases covering management, computing, social science and educational databases. The importance of parallel cultures of evaluation will be discussed further in Chapter 5.

Benchmarking

While evidence-based information practice seeks to collect and evaluate comparative research data, benchmarking originated as a comparative management technique which focuses on relevant competitors. It is a technique originally developed by industry in which best practice by one's competitors is studied to improve one's own performance. Benchmarking can improve the customer focus through seeing how others satisfy their customers. In librarianship, libraries can compare themselves with others to effect an improvement in performance. It is, however, difficult to compare services in different institutions which are highly qualitative – enquiries desks are a good example. Measures or benchmarks to use in comparing libraries have to be chosen with care and it can be difficult to find several libraries for which the same set of measures will be appropriate and the best benchmarking partners have to be chosen to give the exercise credibility.

Benchmarking is a continuous process designed to generate improvements. There are five stages (Creaser, 2001):

1. Measure your services and select the aspects to be benchmarked. Do not benchmark areas which cannot be changed if change is indicated.

2. Find suitable benchmarking partners. For benchmarking to be effective the philosophy, aims and objectives of the partner organisations must be similar, at least in respect of the services under consideration.

3. Identify best practice. It is important to be aware that what constitutes 'best practice' in one situation may not be 'best practice' in another. Appropriate choice of benchmarking partners should take care of this.

4. Discover the service features and procedures which give rise to 'best practice' and change your own where appropriate.

5. Measure your service to assess the impact of the exercise and move on.

A pre-existing culture of evaluation is fundamental to the above processes. Some pre-existing degree of commonality, usually found in the organisational structure makes the task of finding comparators easier. This is notably the case in higher education although there are divides, such as between the pre- and post-1992 universities. In public library services this can generally be achieved by seeking groups within the traditional local government sectors. Public library services also have the advantage of having a statutory basis to the service which provides common ground between library authorities so that comparisons can be made with confidence. There are obvious areas where this is less applicable, such as special and school library services. In the latter case, school library services are not provided on any statutory basis outside Northern Ireland and no two school library services offer the same range of services. There are also no nationally agreed guidelines as to what services should be provided. In such cases the best approach is to look for guidance at international standards, such as ISO 11620.

Benchmarking conventionally uses a variety of methods both quantitative and qualitative (Hart, 2002):

- *Mystery shopping*: In this technique an investigator poses as a member of the public to use and evaluate a service. The success of the method depends on a strong and open relationship between the investigator and investigated. It is essential that both parties agree in advance the criteria for measurement and the reporting back of potentially sensitive results. Although the technique can be used extremely successfully, preparation is both essential and very time-consuming as mutually agreed criteria for assessment have to be worked out. Enquiry desk services have been evaluated in this way both in public and university libraries but it can also be used in the electronic environment to evaluate web services off campus.

- *Exit interviews*: In this method, backroom or offsite staff interview users after they have left the library outside the physical boundaries of the library. It tends to provide frank views and a realistic picture of service provision. As with other qualitative methods it gives the respondent an opportunity to spontaneously air issues about matters other than the subject of the enquiry. It can also be used to evaluate enquiry services. Like mystery shopping, it is always time-consuming and there is always the possibility of interview and respondent bias.

- *Behavioural study*: This is in fact observation, as described above, and all the points made there hold good. For the purposes of benchmarking, the method is useful for investigating 'people flows' – the movements and activities of users. The method is time-consuming and could perhaps be simplified by using videotaping although it is important to be aware of data protection issues.

- *Measuring process times*: These are essentially counting exercises and can be done with routine activities susceptible to quantitative methods like speed and accuracy of reshelving. In the case of reshelving time, book tracking slips can be put into books to quantify the time taken to complete various stages of the process, similar to route card surveys which have been used in the past to estimate speed of acquisition and cataloguing procedures.

The planning and implementing of these methods and interpretation of the results is a highly skilled and expert activity and not just a matter of asking users for a subjective opinion.

Thanks to the emergence of large-scale, reliable databases of information, such as those held by the Library and Information Statistics Unit, statistical benchmarking to compare performance is also possible. This entails only statistical comparisons and, like most forms of evaluation, has only one goal: the improvement of library services. It does not give information on impacts and outcomes and it is not always possible to know what lies behind the changes reported by individual institutions from year to year (Creaser, 2004). Public libraries have their own benchmarking club (*http://www.ipfbenchmarking.net/ leisure/publiclibraries/default.asp*) maintained by CIPFA which is being relaunched at the time of writing. The current emphasis is to address the demands of the DCMS 'Framework for the Future', the development of action plans, toolkits and practical guidance to improve performance and the continued dissemination of emerging and established best practice. The service is based around a web-based hub of best practice and information services, including an indexed, searchable database of best practice, a number of Public Library Standards (PLS) comparison tools, plus the addition of further relevant toolkits and practical guidance during the year. These are provided along with a forum for all members to share and discuss best practice with each other and a panel of experts.

Software to support survey and evaluation work

A wide range of software is available to support survey and evaluation work. Software packages were originally offline products intended only for data input and analysis. Paper survey forms had to be laboriously keyed in or scanned using an expensive machine. Nowadays web-based packages are widely available and can be administered on library computers, portals or by e-mail. Historically, it has been argued that such methods were unsound because they produced a biased sample, consisting only of the IT literate. In education, such an argument is no longer justified, as the computer pervades all aspects of the lives of both staff and students, and basic IT literacy skills are taken for granted. Such an approach is particularly appropriate in special libraries, where all staff have access to e-mail. In public libraries, however, where high levels of computer literacy cannot be expected of all users, paper administration still has its advantages and staff can explain the purpose behind the questionnaire while handing it out.

A general Web search will yield plenty of information about survey software and a more careful search of specific library websites will give more precise evidence of good practice. A useful introduction, 'Library Surveys & Questionnaires', compiled by Joe Ryan can be found at *http://web.syr.edu/~jryan/infopro/survey.html*. It includes links to specific examples of web surveys and also several widely used survey instruments.

In deciding which is the most appropriate, a number of criteria can be applied:

- Are there clear instructions?
- Are demonstrations available?
- Is it easy to carry out cross tabulations, for example, usage of a specific service by gender?
- Is the survey form easy to design?
- Can it deal with free text questions?
- Is it easy for someone with limited IT expertise to use?
- Is support from dedicated IT staff needed?
- Can it be used for e-mail and web surveys?
- Is training available?
- Are multi-user site licenses available?
- Can the data collected be exported to a statistical package, such as SPSS, for further analysis?

Using any software package necessarily involves some learning, and the more complex the package, the more learning is needed. More complex packages produce more specialised outputs, but it is necessary to ask if this will be needed in practice.

Packages available include SNAP (*http://www.snapsurveys .com/*), a suite of integrated software programs for questionnaire design, publication, data collection and analysis. It consists of a core product, Snap Professional, currently in version 8, which is for questionnaire design and analysis and it is fairly easy to learn and use. There are additional modules which can be used for publishing the questionnaire on the Web or via e-mail and it can also be administered on PDAs. Web-based publishing may require some IT support. Campus licences can be bought. It is very much a market research oriented product and represents a reasonable compromise between a wide range of features and relative ease of use.

Additionally, Survey Monkey (*http://www.surveymonkey .com/*) is a simple, easy to use and inexpensive product which allows surveys to be quickly designed and mounted on the Web. Data are analysed and updated as results come in so the user can concentrate on interpretation of the results. Cross-tabulation can easily be done and it is possible to keyword search free text responses. Results can be exported to Excel or SPSS for further analysis.

Software packages are also available to support qualitative data analysis with the intention of reducing the drudgery of sorting and coding complex qualitative data. It does, however, use technical processing methods to analyse data more suited to rigorous intellectual enquiry. A good example which has been used by librarians is QSR*NUDIST (*http://www.scolari.co.uk/frame.html?http://www.scolari.co.uk/ qsr/qsr_n4.htm*). It offers 'a complete toolkit for rapid coding, thorough exploration and rigorous management and analysis'. It is most useful in dealing with large volumes of qualitative data.

Toolkits

Toolkits are essentially checklists of activities to help practitioners to evaluate their performance and plan improvements, and are found in various areas of professional activity. They usually draw on pre-existing practice or published standards.

The eVALUEd toolkit (*http://www.evalued.uce.ac.uk/*), for example, is designed to support information services staff in higher education institutions with the evaluation of electronic information services (EIS). The toolkit takes a user-focused approach to the evaluation of EIS mainly through the use of qualitative data collection methods. The toolkit was developed from evidence-based research and is divided into four sections:

- *How to evaluate EIS*: This provides information about the evaluation process with a step-by-step guide to all elements of the evaluation process, including planning and conducting an evaluation and making effective use of evaluation findings.

- *EIS evaluation themes*: Information and tips to help the user evaluate particular themes relating to EIS, e.g. impact on learning, teaching and research, user support, outcomes assessment and access. This section allows the user to go straight to tools related to a specific theme.

- *Tools archive*: A range of tools, such as questionnaires, interview questions, checklists and statistics for each evaluation theme.

- *Custom tools*: This allows the user to create tools based on the standard resources provided in the toolkit.

There are also a variety of site resources including case studies.

An example from school libraries is the DfES funded Self Evaluation Toolkit (*http://www.teachernet.gov.uk/teachingandlearning/resourcematerials/schoollibraries/*). It consists of self-evaluation frameworks for primary and secondary school libraries/learning resource centres which were produced by the DfES in conjunction with the School Libraries Working Group. They provide school librarians with a clear way of assessing the quality of what they provide and measuring outcomes, as well as providing evidence of achievement and identifying areas that could be improved. They also provide practical advice and suggestions for improving the way that the library supports pupil learning. There are two toolkits:

- Improve your library: a self-evaluation process for primary schools.

- Improve your library: a self-evaluation process for secondary school libraries and learning resource centres.

Further education colleges in Scotland have their own quality toolkit called The Library Service Development Toolkit (*http://www.slainte.org.uk/files/pdf/fenet/toolkit03.pdf*) launched in 2004. It follows on from a set of standards, published in 1997, *Libraries in Scottish Further Education Colleges: Standards for Performance and Resourcing* (2nd edn). It aims to provide information and support to enable college libraries and learning centre managers in Scotland to carry out self-evaluation. The toolkit consists of seven indicators against which to evaluate the library and information function. The toolkit reflects the changes which have been made in further education libraries in Scotland since 1997 with the increasing adoption of e-learning, advances in ICT and digital online resources, and the information professionals' role in the development and creation of online services.

The quality indicators in the toolkit help learning resource service managers to:

- judge the quality of performance against a set of criteria;
- identify development needs and priorities;
- highlight best practice;
- reach decisions about the overall pattern of strength and weakness in the service performance.

The indicators are:

- *Learning Resources Organisation*, which covers developing systems for shared resources including system development, interoperability and collaborative collection development.
- *Staffing*, which looks at staffing arrangements including qualifications and opportunities for staff development.
- *ICT integration*, which addresses electronic access and managing digital resources including system interface, remote services and using recognised metadata standards.
- *User support*, including the range and balance of resources offered and service support for a range study and attendance patterns.
- *Accessibility*, covering information and assistance, maximising access and access agreements.
- *Inclusiveness*, which looks at complying with legislation and promoting diversity.
- *Quality assurance and improvement* covers suitable structures, systems and procedures to apply quality.

The quality indicators can be used to evaluate at the four levels of performance which are used by HMI:

- Very good: major strengths;
- Good: strengths outweigh weaknesses;
- Fair: some important weaknesses;
- Unsatisfactory: major weaknesses.

All the methodologies described above have advantages and disadvantages; some of them are extremely time-consuming and some are best applied to specialist situations. For libraries with limited resources it is best, at least initially, to opt for a mixture of simple qualitative and quantitative methods based around a regular satisfaction survey to give essential statistical data, supplemented by focus groups to understand the thinking that informs the survey results. A basic satisfaction survey can, in turn, be supplemented by other surveys to collect more data on specific issues, while focus groups can be supplemented by other qualitative methods to clarify users' thinking on particularly complex issues. Although there is apparently a clear distinction between quantitative methods and qualitative ones, they may subsist together within such methodologies as observation and benchmarking.

4

General satisfaction survey instruments

Overview surveys, often administered annually or every two years are widely used in libraries and this chapter discusses some of the most widely used methods. They originated in the early 1990s, one of the most influential examples being that contained in Nancy Van House et al. (1990), which was adopted by SCONUL in the UK. The surveys are often called satisfaction surveys. Satisfaction has been defined by Hernon and Whitman (2001) as a sense of contentment that arises from an *actual* experience in relation to an expected experience. The degree to which expectations conform to or deviate from experience is the pivotal determinant of satisfaction. Customer satisfaction measures a customer's immediate and subjective experience with a specific service encounter. Hernon and Whitman give examples of questionnaires for public and academic libraries which can be used with little modification. They make it easy for customers to report satisfaction and their particular concerns. The resulting assessment data provide the basis for an evaluation of how well the service is achieving its mission and service goals. The evaluation, together with a focus on service quality, can result in recommended action to correct service problems and can even point to the need to revise the mission or service goals.

This approach has attracted its critics (Walters, 2003). Satisfaction surveys assume that users have the necessary expertise to make accurate assessments of quality and that perceptions serve as valid indicators of objective conditions. There is certainly some truth in the former point. The more complex the service, the more difficult users will find in commenting usefully. When asked to list favourite electronic information databases, for example, users will often list general websites instead because they do not understand the difference. In both higher education and public libraries users are constrained by their lack of experience of using libraries other than their own. In higher education, especially, services are a ladder of complexity and undergraduates may never experience higher-level services aimed mainly at academics and researchers. The very term *customer* is contentious. Library users have duties to the service they use which are controlled by regulations and in higher education, even disciplinary procedures. These sit alongside the users' rights and the library 'customer' cannot be viewed as the same as a supermarket customer. Unlike retail services, libraries operate under resource constraints and the quality of service offered has to be viewed in this light. Librarians should also use the data they collect themselves, such as journal citation data, use data, such as circulation statistics, reshelving surveys and interlibrary loan data.

In reality, some of these criticisms can be, at least partially, answered by the procedures that have been developed by well established instruments.

General surveys in UK higher education

A short questionnaire on survey activity in UK academic libraries in December 2003 showed that at least 62 carry out user surveys. Sixty per cent of respondents carry out annual surveys, which, if carried out over a period of years, creates valuable longitudinal data, which can help to counteract the charge of subjectivity if a consistent picture can be built up over a period of years. A range of survey instruments are used. The most popular is the Libra package provided by Priority Research which, at the time of writing, is being completely updated into a web-based survey instrument, called e-inform. This is followed by LibQUAL+™ (described below) and a variety of in-house packages. At least 16 libraries use adapted versions of the SCONUL satisfaction survey template (discussed below). Surveys are increasingly web-based as this has been found to produce better response rates. The general survey is often supplemented by surveys on specific issues. An issue of increasing importance is whether or not the library survey should remain independent or be subsumed in a wider university survey run by an evaluation agency within the university (see Chapter 5) (West, 2004). General surveys also have to be sufficiently flexible to cope with converged or merged services by including, for example, questions about satisfaction with computer use.

The SCONUL template user satisfaction survey

The original SCONUL template user satisfaction survey appeared in 1996 (Revill and Ford, 1996) for use in UK academic libraries and was designed to succeed the questionnaire based on the work of Van House and associates (West, 2001). The take-up of this questionnaire was less than had been hoped, partly because it was very library oriented, with minimal coverage of such topics as networked information services and PC systems used by students. The revised 2001 template arose out of the work of the SCONUL Working Group on User Satisfaction and was an attempt to update Revill and Ford (1996). The template was again updated in 2005 and now has two variants, depending on whether or not the library forms part of a converged service (*http://www.sconul.ac.uk/activities/ performance/surveys/templates.html*).

The templates are not intended as a standalone instrument but should be used with other survey and evaluation methodologies and library management data of the kind outlined above. The templates can be analysed by most statistical packages, depending on the complexity of outputs required. The questionnaires can be modified and extended for local use. Piloting the original survey showed difficulties in using the data for interinstitutional comparisons because the same services might be presented, managed and used differently in different institutions. The opportunity to build up a longitudinal picture over several years seemed more useful. Reasons given for adopting the template included:

- It has longitudinal value and can be used over time. Ratings can be plotted to build up an evolving view of services.

- The data collected can be incorporated into library performance indicators.

- It is easy to use and is suitable for annual administration.

- It identifies priorities for action. A wide variation between the importance and satisfaction rating for a particular service is an indication of the need to take remedial action.

- It identifies subgroup agendas (cross-tabulation). Using the demographic data (age, mode of attendance etc.) it is possible to cross-tabulate the satisfaction of particular categories of user with specific services.

- Results can be used to inform public relations activity.

- Something new can be learned about the user. Despite continuing concerns about noise and availability of textbooks, satisfaction with new services can be evaluated. The introduction of electronic services over the past ten years is a good example of this.

The current Library Satisfaction Survey template (not for a converged service) questionnaire is divided into six sections (See Appendix A):

1. Demographic data about the respondent (questions 1–6). This now includes gender and ethnicity.

2. Frequency of use (questions 7–9): frequency of use of a main library or branch, frequency of visits to preferred library and frequency of accessing library and information services via a computer.

3. Success in using key services either by visiting the library in person or via a computer (questions 10–11): success for four key activities (visiting in person) and five key activities (visiting remotely).

4. Satisfaction and importance of key services and facilities (question 12): the respondent is invited to indicate the importance they attach to the same 17 issues. This is an important feature because it gives some idea of users' expectations of particular services. Users with low expectations of a service might be pleasantly surprised if it is delivered well. Alternatively if users have high expectations of a service they may be critical of any

deficiencies. Access to sufficient copies of basic textbooks and the reliability of computers are good examples of this. Expressed satisfaction with a service may just mean that it is not used very much.

5. Overall satisfaction (question 13): users are invited to express on overall view on their satisfaction level with the service.

6. Section 14 is a free text box allowing users to make any comments or suggestions they think appropriate.

The survey for a converged service (Information Services Satisfaction Survey) does not differ a great deal but includes additional issues, such as satisfaction and importance relating to e-mail and Blackboard (virtual learning environment).

Creaser (2005) has undertaken a pilot study on the potential for using the original SCONUL template (not for a converged service) for benchmarking purposes. This showed that the nine participants had not all used the standard template in its entirety. Some had omitted questions or parts of questions while others had added questions for local use. Not all participants had administered the survey in the approved manner. Average scores were calculated for each of the rating scale items in the survey, although, because the participants were such a diverse group, the results were of doubtful value. In the results, the importance ratings given to individual items tended to be rather higher than the satisfaction levels. The highest rating for any item was the importance of the range of books at one participating library where 92 per cent of respondents rated this 'very' important. In overall satisfaction, no library performed particularly poorly. The final question in the SCONUL template is 'overall the library provides a good service to me'. Fewer than 10 per cent of respondents disagreed with this statement in any library. The pilot study showed that the SCONUL template could be used for benchmarking purposes provided that comparators are chosen carefully and the survey methodology is applied consistently.

LibQUAL+™

While the SCONUL template is a UK product, LibQUAL+™ (*http://www.libqual.org/Information/index.cfm*) has become an international, web-based service which allows other institutions to benchmark against each other and also uses the gap analysis model. It is the outcome of a research partnership between the American Association of Research Libraries (ARL) and the Texas A&M University Libraries to develop a programme of systematic service quality assessment from the library user perspective. More than 700 libraries have used it since the original pilot took place across 13 libraries in 2000. LibQUAL+™ is a regrounded version of the original (Cook et al., 2004) 22-item SERVQUAL tool for the library environment (Kyrillidou and Heath, 2001). It seeks to measure the gap between user expectations and perceptions of service delivery. Extensive qualitative and quantitative iterative research methods have been employed to reground the protocol which, like the original SERVQUAL, ended up with 22 items in the 2004 and 2005 annual implementation. These 22 items measure three dimensions of service quality:

- effect of service (questions concerning the effectiveness of library staff);
- information control (including the availability of resources and the ability to access them);
- library as place (questions on the physical environment).

The 22 survey items are measured with three scales for (a) users' minimum, (b) perceived, and (c) desired levels of service quality.

Participants may also select five questions to ask locally and there is a box for open-ended comments from users regarding their concerns and suggestions

LibQUAL+™ has evolved into a rather extensive suite of services that serves the following goals to:

- foster a culture of excellence in providing library service;
- help libraries better understand user perceptions of library service quality;
- collect and interpret library user feedback systematically over time;
- provide libraries with comparable assessment information from peer institutions;
- identify best practices in library service;
- enhance library staff members' analytical skills for interpreting and acting on data.

These aims are not too different from the SCONUL template. However, LibQUAL+™ data are interpreted rather differently. Scores on perceptions can be compared against scores on what is reported to be minimally acceptable services and what is reported to be desired service. This is called the 'zone of tolerance' interpretation framework. Second statistical norms may be used to characterise factually what percentage of users of institutions generate lower perception ratings. This can be used to identify specific user groups who feel dissatisfied with the service (Cook et al., 2004). Users in individual institutions are invited to complete the survey, the URL for the library's web form being distributed via e-mail. Respondents complete the survey form and their answers are sent to a central database. The data are analysed and presented to the individual library in reports describing the users' desired, perceived, and minimum expectations of service.

LibQUAL+™ was first piloted in the UK in 2003 with 20 participants (Town, 2004a) but the questionnaire was modified to include questions on:

- access to photocopying and print facilities;
- main text and reading needed;
- provision for information skills training;
- helpfulness in dealing with users' IT problems;
- availability of subject specialist assistance.

Although the pilot was successfully administered, response rates participants achieved were below those achieved by previously used satisfaction surveys. Aggregated results drawn from all participants highlight some fairly familiar issues where performance fell below users' minimum expectations. These were in the area of information resource provision and availability – print and electronic journal collections, and needed printed library materials. The overall picture was of well-regarded library staff providing a good service but unable, probably for economic reasons, to fully satisfy the demand for information resources. Cranfield University which had previous experience of the SCONUL template compared results for both. Using LibQUAL+™, no service area was found to fall below minimum expectations, but it was possible to identify an agenda for improvement from those questions receiving the lowest adequacy mean. Access to information (including access to print and electronic sources and opening hours) and personal control (including website access, reliability of hardware and off-site access) were the areas identified, as widely found elsewhere. LibQUAL+™ achieved a response rate of 14 per cent compared with 21 per cent using the SCONUL template. Both questionnaires use a gap methodology – perceived versus minimum and desired (LibQUAL+™) and satisfaction versus importance (SCONUL template); results from both bring out the same issues and provide a similar agenda for improvement. Areas where performance is high are the same in both. Participants in the pilot were broadly satisfied with the exercise despite concerns about low response rates. The uses to which LibQUAL+™ results are put do not differ from other instruments – planning and identifying service improvements – although there was some concern about the volume of statistical data created.

Glasgow University Library

LibQUAL+™ continues to be used in the UK (54 institutions since 2003). A good example of a satisfied participant is Glasgow University Library (*http://www.lib.gla.ac.uk/ libqual/*) which has applied the survey in 2003, 2004 and 2005 (see Appendix B). Users are divided into undergraduate, postgraduate and academic and research staff although results from all three are also aggregated together. The 2003 survey yielded the following data. In terms of general satisfaction participants were asked to rate the service on a scale of 1–9 in the following categories:

- Their satisfaction with the way in which they are treated at the library: rated 7.07.

- Their satisfaction with the library support for their learning, research and/or teaching needs: rated 6.54.

- The overall quality of service provided by the library: rated 6.93.

Postgraduate students were least satisfied on the above three points and academic/research staff were most satisfied.

Analysis of the service adequacy gap scores (SAGs = perceived service level minus minimum service level), from the 25 core questions indicated that undergraduates seemed easiest to please and postgraduate students the hardest. They wanted a higher-level service for the provision of journal collections, printed materials and electronic collections. However in the important effect of service area (satisfaction with staff), the minimum expectations of all three categories of user were exceeded.

The continuing importance of the library as physical space was emphasised in the library as a place rating. Again, using the service adequacy gap scores, postgraduates were least satisfied wanting both more individual and group study space. The library had already increased group study space but also improved the booking system as a result of this criticism. The growing importance of off-campus access was noted by all users. All categories wanted better access to electronic resources from home or office but postgraduates expressed this need most strongly.

There were also questions about frequency of use of services which showed the library website to be used daily by approximately 30 per cent of participants and search engines by approximately 50 per cent of participants. Resources within the library are used by approximately 30 per cent of participants daily. Fewer than 5 per cent admitted to not using either virtual or physical library resources, which suggests a high level of market penetration.

The 2004 results suggested some improvement with general satisfaction showing an improvement in all three areas measured, although postgraduate students were still the least satisfied. There was an improvement in participants' perceptions about library staff with undergraduates and postgraduates both rating the library staff more highly than in 2003. In terms of library as place, both undergraduates and postgraduates rated it above their minimum expectations, although there are continuing concerns about the provision of quiet space for individual work. However, the library has zoned every area in the building for acceptable noise levels and also undertaken a refurbishment programme to address this issue.

Frequency of usage of resources showed a growth in the use of the library website, search engines and physical library resources with market penetration approaching 100 per cent.

Comparing the surveys of 2003 and 2004, a longitudinal picture of improvement emerges with the library identifying strengths and areas for improvement, monitoring services usage and identifying issues for the longer term, such as off-campus access.

London School of Economics & Political Science library

Some UK academic libraries, however, use their own in-house instrument as they feel it gives them more control over the questions they can select and changes can be made if necessary, although this naturally involves more local work. A good example is the questionnaire used at the London School of Economics & Political Science which runs an annual student satisfaction survey. It is held during the second term, a reflection of common practice, and since 2002 the survey has been run online. It is distributed via e-mail to all LSE students, and is also available on the library website. In 2005 staff began using survey software from Bristol Online Surveys (*http://www.surveys.bris.ac.uk*).

Although LSE staff have considered using standard templates (such as SCONUL and LIBQUAL) they decided to maintain the in-house approach because it offers the freedom to define questions and it allows users' needs to set the priorities. The survey measures both importance and satisfaction like the SCONUL template and the same wording is maintained each year, helping staff to compare the results with previous years. Both closed and open questions are asked. Each year a prize draw incentive is offered to encourage completion. This seems to work. In 2005 an iPod mini was offered which generated the highest response rate since the survey was begun.

Library managers use the detailed results in their operational planning, and each year changes and improvements are made as a result of the survey results. A valuable feature of the exercise is that information about changes is communicated back to the users.

The questionnaire has 34 questions divided into five sections, including the usual personal and ethnic information and the standard question about general satisfaction. Unusually, users are invited to make free text comments about specific issues, including telephone enquiries and self-issue of books. There are also questions about the use of other academic libraries, queuing times at all service points, speed of reshelving and both printed and electronic course packs. Such a sophisticated instrument offers excellent scope for data collection and analysis.

The German experience

In Germany, a general survey instrument has been used in higher education with the specific aim of facilitating interinstitutional comparisons (benchmarking) despite the problem of the different circumstances in each institution. (Mundt, 2003). In the spring and summer of 2001, all 15 university libraries in North Rhine Westphalia in north-western Germany decided to complement their existing benchmarking data by conducting a joint user satisfaction survey across 34 different libraries and branches. A commercial organisation, infas, was employed to develop a survey design, coordinate data collection and analyse the data. To ensure consistency, all libraries used the same survey methodology and input and analysis of the collected data was done by infas staff to ensure neutrality in interpretation. In addition, it was agreed in advance that all comparative data would be anonymised. As each library had different data about its users, it was decided to distribute the questionnaire in paper form in each library; 22,500 questionnaires were distributed in total, proportionate to the size of the population served in each library. As only seven of the 15 participating libraries had conducted a user satisfaction survey before, care was taken to ensure that the same distribution methods were used in each library and questionnaires were distributed over the same period in each library.

The questionnaire itself had a conventional service or product focused structure similar to but more detailed than the SCONUL template. Users were asked to rate their satisfaction with 14 services on a five-point scale.

The results produced a fairly familiar repertoire of concerns. Critical service gaps were found to be Internet access, seating, photocopying facilities and the short loan collection. Statistical analysis of the data showed variations in users' attitudes to similar services. Two libraries with similar opening hours produced different levels of satisfaction among users – something which requires exploring local factors to uncover the reasons. In general, however, longer opening hours on weekday evenings had a more positive effect on customer satisfaction than extended opening hours at weekends.

In general, the participating libraries went to some trouble to disseminate the results; 14 out of 15 used various methods to communicate results with staff which resulted in a healthy climate of discussion among staff about service quality and how it could be improved. Additionally, nine libraries reported the results to university management.

Fourteen libraries quickly initiated activities to effect improvements, although only nine had set up a prioritised list of activities and there were only a few cases of systematic benchmarking. Those libraries with quality focused project teams responded more quickly.

Analysis of open-ended questions in the questionnaire suggested that users were likely to assess their own service on the basis of concrete experience of other libraries, something also found in the UK in cities with several universities.

In 2002, the survey was revised and adapted for libraries of the universities of applied sciences in North Rhine Westphalia and was scheduled to be used more widely in Germany in 2004.

The public library experience

In the UK, general satisfaction surveys for public libraries are a national standard which grew out of the Audit Commission's Citizens' Charter exercise in 1992. Conventional statistics were found to be unsuitable to assess how well libraries provided materials and information to the public. Surveys of users which asked specific questions about satisfaction with services seemed to be the answer. Following a large-scale pilot in 1993 and further work, a National Standard for undertaking surveys of users in UK public libraries was launched in late 1994. This established a common base on which public library authorities could compare their results and a forum for the development of visitor surveys.

Public library PLUS surveys

As indicated above, the origins of PLUS go back some ten years as the Committee on Public Library Statistics, the steering group which, at that time, had responsibility under the auspices of the Chartered Institute of Public Finance and Accountancy to gather information from library authorities in the UK, carried out a series of pilot surveys. The main factor at that time was to capture the success rate of an individual's ability to find a specific book or books of choice. To this day, the structure of the questionnaire has changed very little. The questionnaire is broken down into four sections as follows: your activity today, the outcome of your visit, how you rate the services provided and finally, about you. Although some of the sections have expanded over the years, for example, to include basic information about ICT provision and capture of ethnic and disability data, the basic shape has changed little. In its current format the questionnaire is now six pages long.

Ownership of the PLUS questionnaire and methodology moved away from the Committee on Public Library Statistics in 1997 following the launch in 1996. A series of steering groups made up of the library authorities who pay subscription fees for its upkeep now meet on a regular basis to review the methodologies and to see how the questionnaire keeps pace with the demands on library services. The group specifically charged with looking after PLUS, following the Best Value surveys of 2003, began work on redeveloping the questionnaire to take into account a number of themes. This includes reader development and other similar initiatives where the emphasis on outcome is not solely concerned with finding book(s), nor where the satisfaction is solely concerned with a snapshot in time.

PLUS has become the de facto standard for conducting surveys in libraries across the whole UK. In 2002, An Chomhairle Leabharlanna (The Library Council in Dublin) used PLUS for their survey of 28 library authorities. PLUS was adopted by the Audit Commission for the performance indicators in 1999/2000, and subsequently by the Office of the Deputy Prime Minister for the Best Value Surveys in 2000/01. In 2001/02 the Department for Culture, Media and Sport decided to use results from both the adult and children's surveys as part their requirement for Library Standards. The PLUS survey is presented in Appendix C.

Children's PLUS

The Library and Information Services Council (England) Working Party on Library Services to Children and Young People produced the *Investing in Children* report in 1995. The report recommended a variety of actions and has inspired two extremely important documents. In 1997, the Library Association produced the second edition of its *Guidelines on Public Library Services to Children and Young People*, an essential guide to service planning which addresses the key issues raised in *Investing in Children*.

In addition, the Institute for Public Finance, with assistance from the Association of Senior Children's and Education Librarians, produced Children's PLUS in 1997 (see Appendix D). Since then, Children's PLUS has undergone further development in order to assess the needs of and satisfaction with library services by children and young people. The most recent update took place in 2002, following further pilot work among library users and school children. At the time of writing, a fresh new look is being considered regarding the surveying of children and young people in the community with particular emphasis on Sure Start, ICT and non- or lapsed library use.

The Department for Culture, Media and Sport has recently turned to Children's PLUS as the means by which to apply standards in this area and although dialogue continues regarding the make-up of these standards or indicators, it does emphasise the importance with which this area is viewed. Both the PLUS adult and children's surveys are being revised in 2006.

5

Parallel cultures of evaluation in higher education

In higher education, cultures of evaluation are by no means confined to the library. Since the mid-1990s, evaluation strategies have been developed in many universities to evaluate the student experience as a whole. In addition, funding councils have researched into how the student experience is evaluated and have also directly examined the student experience itself. The term 'evaluation of the student experience' is widely used, but feedback and satisfaction are also used. It is a holistic process examining all aspects of the student experience, although the focus is inevitably on the effectiveness of the teaching experience, while library and other support services tend to be evaluated as contributors to this process. This is not necessarily a bad thing, as librarians must be aware of the role of libraries in the wider world of student support, not just as entities in themselves. The process also tends to emphasise communication and feedback, something not always well handled by librarians. As a method it has advantages and disadvantages. One can be certain that the survey has been carried out expertly and that the data are reliable and can be used for benchmarking purposes. Related areas, such as IT services will probably be included. It is often worth reading report areas relating to other support services and even teaching, as some issues may come up widely, such as the varying demands different subject areas make on teaching and support services. However, the data collected may be limited so there will probably be a need for more specialist surveys. The library, although it may benefit from the process, may have little control over it, especially in key areas, such as the selection and design of questions. The tyranny of the short, easy to complete, one to two pages of A4 questionnaire still holds sway and, even if the library is consulted about the content, it will find itself battling with other departments, some perhaps more influential, to get the questions it wants included. A good example of the problem can be found at: *http://www.shefc.ac.uk/publications/other/student_survey .doc.*

The Scottish funding councils for further and higher education report *Survey of Student Experience 2003* follows on from an earlier report, published in 2001. The survey was based on interviews conducted with over 2,000 students in further and higher education in Scotland. In the results it is possible to distinguish the views of further education students from those in higher education. Notably, larger institutions were under-represented in the survey and higher education students were also under-represented, compared with further education students. The gender balance of students was roughly equal.

Overall, the students reported high levels of satisfaction with their learning experience. Only 3 per cent reported dissatisfaction, half of what it was in 2001. The questionnaire found no difference in satisfaction in terms of sex, age, ethnicity, subject group, year of study or type of study, something which is unlikely to be found in a library-only study. Further education students were more likely to be 'very satisfied' than higher education students, which might suggest that pressures on some services are less great in further education. The only direct library indicator is 'The books you need being available in the libraries' which 60 per cent of students reported as being very important and a further 27 per cent, fairly important. A related indicator for librarians 'Having adequate access to computer facilities' generated almost exactly the same response.

Students were asked to rate ten indicators in order of importance. The top three were:

- number of contact hours (with teaching staff): 44 per cent;
- relevance of course to job: 43 per cent;
- adequate support from teaching staff: 40 per cent.

No support or other issue made it to the top three but two relevant indicators came fourth and fifth:

- availability of books in libraries: 37 per cent;
- computer facilities: 33 per cent.

This shows that issues to do with teaching staff will always rank first but libraries and IT provision are the most important of the support services to students. The study found that availability of books was more likely to be mentioned by higher education than further education students, but that this was less likely to be an issue with first-year students. More students were dissatisfied with the availability of books than any other aspect of the learning experience. While 87 per cent considered the availability of books to be important, only 65 per cent expressed satisfaction with provision. Interestingly, similar levels of concern were expressed about careers and job information.

Students were given the opportunity to complain about specific support facilities. Childcare was the cause of most complaints (73) followed by accommodation and building issues (44), followed by libraries (31), a reflection, presumably of the attention libraries now give to customer care issues.

This survey is useful because it gives libraries a sense of place within the institution as the most important support service and the low number of complaints it attracts. However, there is no useful distinction in response by stakeholder group. Where are part-time students, for example? And why is the availability of books the only indicator recorded when it is itself a complex issue breaking down into general reading and key undergraduate texts, up-to-dateness of edition, adequacy of number of copies and availability on the shelves at the time sought.

The study can usefully be compared with the Book Marketing Limited (2003) study published at about the same time, which reported on interviews with 750 students, conducted on 27 campuses. Interviewees were split equally by sex, old or new university and there was a fairly even spread by subject. This showed that the sources of information students were using at the time, in descending order, were books owned by the students themselves, handouts, books borrowed and the Internet, which was used, on average, for three hours per week. Other electronic sources were much less significant; 80 per cent of respondents were found to use their library at least once a week. Books were still generally seen as the fundamental resource outside lectures, although it was recognised that there was a rising demand to study parts of books rather than whole texts, which presumably has implications for the future of text digitisation strategy. Here an expert study with a stronger focus on the same performance issue has produced more useful data.

The Cooke report was published in 2002 (*http://www .hefce.ac.uk/pubs/hefce/2002/02_15.htm*). It identifies the categories of data, information and judgments about the quality and standards of teaching and learning, which should be available within higher education institutions and those which should be published. Two principles are identified: meeting public information needs, so that all stakeholders, and especially students can obtain information which is up to date, consistent and reliable, and second, lightness of touch, so that the burden on universities is reduced to the minimum, consistent with proper accountability and meeting users' information needs. The implication is that each university should have a student satisfaction evaluation programme which regularly reviews all the services it provides. This should include information on students' satisfaction with their experience of library services and IT support as well as such areas as academic and tutorial guidance, physical environment and quality of teaching. Publications should include feedback from current students collected through local surveys 'undertaken on a more consistent basis than now'. It has had some effect. West's (2004) survey of surveys noted that 'a small number of universities may be subsuming their library user survey into a more general institutional student survey'. Higher education libraries, he noted, 'may possibly face difficult decisions'.

Brennan and Williams (2004) have usefully summarised the available feedback mechanisms, both quantitative and qualitative. These include questionnaires, student representation on local and institutional committees, staff–student liaison committees, the lecture or seminar, the tutorial, structured discussion groups, including focus groups and 'other informal mechanisms'. Each method has advantages and disadvantages. In higher education, questionnaires may be affected by the timing of the distribution and whether they are distributed in the classroom or by some other means. Student representation, in whatever form, cannot be relied upon to be truly representative of the whole student body. Consequently, most institutions use a range of qualitative and quantitative methods. Nottingham Trent University recommends additional techniques including log books, informal chats, student diaries and suggestion boxes in addition to the conventional questionnaires and focus groups. A combination of questionnaires, student representation, and staff–student liaison committees represents common practice in most institutions. Structured discussion groups are less common because they require staff training to be effective. Some institutions have used focus groups to structure and improve evaluation mechanisms themselves.

In higher education, the module is the most common level for collecting questionnaire feedback. The justification for this is that the module is closest to the student experience and a focus on the module is more likely to ensure relatively rapid improvements. However, feedback on individual modules does not give a full picture of the student experience. Topics for inclusion in the questionnaire usually include 'use of learning resources and other specialist facilities' but, in practice, this usually means a couple of questions about textbook availability and opening hours.

Qualitative methods have the conventional advantages and disadvantages. Students are represented on institutional committees and staff–student liaison committees, as well as structured discussion groups of one kind or another organised for specific purposes. Student representatives sitting on appropriate committees are potentially an important channel of communication between staff and students. The reality is somewhat different. It can be difficult to recruit interested and enthusiastic students and they need to be trained to carry out their duties efficiently. They may represent their own concerns rather than those of the wider student body and they may be relatively unknown to other students. Teaching staff may not value their role very highly. However, there are advantages. They give students the opportunity to make a direct input into decision making. They allow students to comment on planned developments and not just historical issues. Communication is two-way, interactive and instantaneous. It is also cheap. From the librarians' point of view, these mechanisms, especially staff–student liaison committees, can be a disappointment as they tend to focus on a few well-known issues, such as library environment, opening hours and access to sufficient copies of up-to-date textbooks. Rather more promising from the librarians' point of view are structured discussion groups called for specific purposes in which the librarian can take the initiative both in organising and identifying the issues for discussion. This is particularly useful for a service which is still under development or needs tweaking. Students may be able to supply the insights which can contribute to enhanced understanding of the use being made of the service and how it can be improved.

Action on feedback really depends on whether a committee needs to be involved in the decision-making process. Many issues can be actioned directly by the library, and if the library has a reasonably sensitive evaluation programme it is unlikely that the issues will come out of the blue. Rather, it is more likely to be part of a process of triangulation where the same issue has been independently identified by several evaluation mechanisms. Committee involvement will usually imply larger, more policy oriented issues, which might require a resource commitment. Whatever decision is taken it should be recorded and monitored.

Probably the worst handled aspect of any programme of student evaluation is feedback and dissemination. A failure to feed back to students the outcomes of processes in which they were involved in the first place can lead to widespread cynicism about the whole evaluation process. It is difficult to identify a single mechanism which will reach all students and several may be necessary, something which can be time-consuming. Reports can be published on departmental noticeboards and on portals. It is important for the library to take the initiative by publishing results on its own website or by putting up posters in the library. Contributing articles to the student newspaper and university in-house publications are other possibilities. The library should also develop good relations with student representatives and encourage them to report library related matters back to the committees on which they sit.

Examples of good practice

A good example of a centralised student satisfaction survey programme is the Centre for Research into Quality at the University of Central England in Birmingham (*http://www.uce.ac.uk/crq/ucestudentsat.htm*). It has been producing surveys of students' perceptions since the mid-1990s and most of its reports, except the most current ones, are available online at the above URL. Because the studies are methodologically sophisticated and therefore reliable, they can be used for comparative purposes, most usefully perhaps by 1992 universities. Surveys are carried out online. The most current report available online at the time of writing is that published in 2004 (*http://www.uce.ac.uk/crq/ucestudentsat2004.htm*). This showed that while students were generally satisfied with the service, there were problems in fairly familiar areas. Law and social science students considered the availability of recommended course materials to be unsatisfactory and were dissatisfied with the supply of multiple copies of core textbooks. Most other students were satisfied or barely satisfied with these aspects. Helpfulness of library staff was generally highly rated as was opening hours. Most students rated noise levels as satisfactory apart from law and social science students and those on certain categories of part-time and non-traditional studies, perhaps reflecting the need these students have for a quiet environment during the brief periods they have for study in the library. Control of the use of mobile phones is an included indicator and this was generally considered adequate. Access to electronic services and usefulness of electronic information services generally rated Bs on the A–E scale used. Trends noted included an increase in satisfaction with the range of books available, the number of up-to-date books and the availability of recommended course material, areas where users are often difficult to satisfy. Helpfulness of library staff has been consistently highly regarded since 1996 which shows what a large quantity of longitudinal data has been built up. Library opening hours have also been rated highly for a long period, since 1997. Satisfaction with the usefulness of electronic information sources has also acquired a longitudinal dimension, having been improving since 2001.

A feature less common in 'academic library' surveys and worth looking at for comparative data are perceptions by age and gender, ethnicity and special needs. This shows, for example, that men are less satisfied than women with the availability of recommended course material and that special needs students rate availability of recommended course material and multiple copies of core textbooks only at category C in the A–E scale.

While the University of Central England programme offers useful information, librarians might feel that it is constrained by its wider remit.

A similar exercise, which uses methodologies comparable to the University of Central England, the Centre for Research and Evaluation, exists at Sheffield Hallam University (*http://www.shu.ac.uk/research/cre/SES/2005/ summary.htm*) and has been conducting student experience surveys since the 2000/01 academic year. Surveys are carried out online and while other agencies within the university are not precluded from carrying out their own surveys, they are expected to follow a standardised methodology. The learning centre is part of the overall student experience survey. Other support services, such as computing facilities and student services are also included. The 2005 survey found that overall general aspects of the learning centre were satisfactory or very satisfactory. Overall, computer based facilities were very satisfactory but availability of PCs at the learning centre was unsatisfactory and very important. All aspects of self-service facilities were very satisfactory. All aspects of other facilities were satisfactory, some were rated unimportant. Generally the study environment was satisfactory, lighting and cleanliness were very satisfactory. Overall, off-campus services were very satisfactory, range and access to e-journals and e-books was satisfactory. Results are given both overall and for the four faculties and although the methodologies are different from library general satisfaction surveys, the same issues emerge. Issues are scored A–E in descending order. 'Getting hold of the books I need for my course' rated a B (satisfactory and very important). Opening hours and 'Helpfulness of learning centre staff' rated an A (very satisfactory and very important). Computer based facilities produced the usual varied picture with 'Availability of PCs at the learning centre' earning Cs (adequate and very important) or Ds (unsatisfactory and very important). However, the learning centre catalogue and 'Access to information databases' earned mainly As. Self-service facilities generally rated As while photocopiers, scanners and printers rated mostly Bs in what can be a difficult maintenance area. Study environment is broken down into no fewer than ten subheadings including such old friends as noise, temperature and signage. Off-campus services is broken down into 11 sections including 'Helpfulness of learning centre staff', 'Catalogue renewals' and 'Learning centre catalogue' which rate mostly As. Issues concerning e-journals and e-books rate mostly Bs. Given the growing importance of off-campus access, this is a useful feature.

Previously, for ten years from 1995, the learning centre undertook annual surveys using the 'Priority Search' survey software and it is instructive to compare methodologies and outcomes. The methodology adopted was the standard practice for those libraries using this software. The process began with a series of staff and student focus groups to establish key areas for further exploration. Focus groups were not run every year, but were a useful source of information to confirm the validity, or otherwise, of library staff perceptions.

The response rate achieved by the university's student experience survey was as low as 12 per cent; the learning centre student survey improved on that total but never exceeded 20 per cent of the total student population. The software was flexible enough for it to be adapted to suit larger or smaller survey groups. Distance learners and postgraduate surveys could be run with minimum customisation and maximum focus, thus ensuring purer data sets for specific communities.

The format of the questionnaire was selected so that additional questions could be inserted when necessary. Those included provided information to be used within the planning process. The response to a question on the potential use of the learning centres during the night (24-hour opening) confirmed staff views that this would be most welcome. In 2002, a pilot for 24-hour opening was run and this has resulted in the continuation of a highly-valued service.

The 'paired comparison' methodology contained within the survey, offered a most useful source of data for planning. In essence, this method allows a number of issues to be judged against others in such a way to elicit the highest priority. In a set of 32 options, each option would be set against two others. If an item was consistently chosen against other options, it indicated a clear priority. These data were used to identify those actions that received the highest resource in subsequent planning.

The university required action plans on an annual basis as part of an annual quality review. The survey was one of three measures used to create this plan, the others being analysis of comments and feedback forms received during the year, and analysis of issues arising from subject based staff–student committees. The action plans were monitored and feedback was provided to users in various formats, including a presentation and display in public areas and reports to faculty academic boards by the information specialists (departmental representatives).

This combined activity created a robust longitudinal dataset from the survey for planning and trend analysis, a set of priorities for planning purposes and a qualitative data set for triangulation. Recent developments have resulted in the learning centre survey being incorporated into the university's student experience survey which is a 'satisfaction – importance' based survey.

This review shows that comparative data from wider programmes of evaluation are of some use in putting the library into a wider context and reviewing some issues not picked up in library surveys, but an adequate range of performance indicators and sufficient level of detail are often lacking. It is important for those planning such programmes to work with librarians to identify a viable range of performance indicators.

Case study: Student Evaluation Project at Glasgow Caledonian University[1]

Origins

The Student Evaluation Project (SEP) was established in August 2001, as a Glasgow Caledonian University (GCU) research project, financed from the Widening Access premium funds received by the Scottish Higher Education Funding Council Grant Funding for the 2001/02 academic session. The project is based in the university's Centre for Research in Lifelong Learning, overseen by an advisory group which involves staff drawn from teaching departments, academic administration and central services/support sections and includes the associate deans for all of the university's academic schools.

Objectives

The main aims of the project are:

- To ensure that GCU has more comprehensive and systematic data regarding the social and educational characteristics of its entrants and their experience while GCU students.

- To provide data which can inform strategy and planning with a view to improving student retention and progression.
- To identify issues to be addressed in improving the student experience, and in providing additional support for students.

Major elements of the project

To date, the project has focused on the following themes and has employed a range of quantitative and qualitative research methods.

Profiling new full-time undergraduate entrants

For the first two cohorts involved in the project, those entering in academic sessions 2001/02 and 2002/03, this involved a self-completion questionnaire being issued to all new full-time undergraduate entrants during their enrolment sessions or alternative sessions as agreed by programme organisers. Although much of the data mirrored that collected via the university registration process, the questionnaires used also provided additional information from respondents in areas such as their choice of university and degree programme, educational and social background, family contact with higher education and student employment. This approach resulted in detailed profiles being generated for over 70 per cent of all first-year new full-time GCU undergraduate entrants over the first two years of the SEP. Since the 2003/04 academic session, the university has employed a web-based self-registration system, which has been modified to incorporate these additional topics and all data are now made available directly to the SEP.

Studies of student satisfaction

Three sets of student satisfaction studies have now been undertaken. These have focused on a number of areas including student use and assessment of central GCU services and facilities, the sources, use and effectiveness of student support systems and their satisfaction with a number of features of their degree programmes. For the first two cohorts, a web-based questionnaire was employed but resulted in unacceptably low response rates. In light of this, a modified approach, employing a machine-readable self-completion questionnaire has been distributed to second, third and fourth level students in the current academic session and has generated responses from over 1,100 students.

Table 5.1 Graduate study – assessment of library

	Strongly agree	Agree	Disagree	Strongly disagree
Library staff were readily available and helpful	19.2	59.8	7.8	1.1
Library resources were sufficient	22.8	51.6	13.5	2.1

Source: Student Evaluation Project survey of 300 graduates, May 2005

Table 5.2 Student satisfaction study – assessment of library facilities and importance rating of library

	Very good	Good	Poor	Very poor
View of GCU library facilities	19.8	52.7	8.4	2.2
Importance of library in supporting student life and development	Very important	Important	Unimportant	
	44.6	41.5	1.7	

Source: Student Evaluation Project survey of 1,150 full-time undergraduates then in Level 2, 3 or 4 of their degree programme, Semester A, Session 2004/05

Tables 5.1 and 5.2 give examples of the views collected from both graduands and undergraduates. While they reflect the fairly general data collected by such studies it is interesting to compare the views of graduands and undergraduates in the question on 'Library resources'/'View of GCU library facilities' which suggests that lengthy contact with the service does not greatly alter the view of it.

Studies of progression and retention

A major element of the project's work has been a longitudinal study of the progression and retention of each student cohort since the 2001/02 session. Here the aim has been to monitor and analyse the progression pathways taken by students during their time at GCU. This has been achieved by tracking each student through their degree programme and downloading the final examination/assessment decisions reached by programme assessment boards at the end of each academic session and merging this information with their detailed personal data generated by the initial profiling exercise conducted by the SEP, as outlined above. To date, this approach has allowed the first 2001/02 cohort to be tracked though three years of their degree programmes and the 2002/03 cohort through two years and has made a significant contribution to the university's understanding of the main factors that influence student progression and retention. This includes the identification and explanation of educational, personal and institutional factors that contribute to differential progression outcomes between GCU student groups. It has also provided a basis upon which GCU policy change can be assessed, such as the impact changes to its examination regulations, which permit students to carry up to two modules from one level to the next, or whether the decision to offer the opportunity for academic consolidation, by allowing 'failing' students to continue at their existing level, actually results in improved progression and retention rates or merely defers problems until a later stage in the student's academic career. While it might seem that progression and retention has no relevance to the evaluation of library services, this has not proved to be the case (Crawford et al., 2004). A study of the usage of electronic information services by school/subject area has shown a hierarchy of usage of electronic services which mirrors progression and retention by school. Making definite statistical comparisons of this kind is difficult as other factors have to be taken into consideration, such as entry qualifications, student commitment and the subject areas' commitment to an innovative learning and teaching agenda. Nevertheless, it is evidence of the library making an impact in conjunction with other factors.

Study of student experience

In the second semester of session 2003/04, the project conducted 25 group interviews, involving around 100 cohort 1 students, designed to gather information on the student experience of GCU and student life in general. The group selection process, which selected some groups from students within a given academic school and others randomly from across the university, was designed to generate findings that were 'school specific' as well as those of more general 'university-wide' interest. This research method was deliberately chosen to be less prescriptive and to allow the 'student's voice' to be heard. It focused on three broad areas of the students' experience:

- the background to their choice of GCU and the degree programme;

- their understanding/explanation of student motivation and commitment;
- their experience of balancing university commitments with their other personal and social commitments.

These discussions have provided some fascinating insights into the diversity of the GCU student body in an era of mass higher education and the complexity of the lives they experience. They also identify the need for a clear institutional recognition of such factors as it develops its teaching and learning strategies.

The library and student experience at GCU

Qualitative studies of student experience at GCU indicate that the library plays a central role in the quality of the student experience at GCU. To date, qualitative studies on student experience carried out by the SEP have not been developed with the library as a key focus. Rather, data regarding the library have been generated on the basis that students themselves regard the library as key to their experience at GCU. These studies illustrate that students have a diversity of opinions regarding the library. Some students have highly positive views of the service, while others are more critical. Some students are quite positive about the library with regard to facilities and opening hours, but are perhaps unsurprisingly critical of library fines, and the short loan service:

> I like how you have opened your library until late on and the fines, the library fines – I suppose that is one thing that I do have a bit of a bone of contention about because I think they are an absolutely outrageous rate.
> Jennifer, female undergraduate

Most students refer to the density of usage of the library, highlighting difficulties of accessing computer facilities and study spaces, and books at peak times:

> I have done [visited the library] once but generally what I have done over the last year is find out the recommended books and looked at the books in the library but they aren't there so I go down to the bookshop and buy it and do the studying at home at my own leisure.
>
> Brian, male mature student

When such issues of access to computers, books and study spaces are raised, students are often quick to note that such issues arise due to a strain on the system. Such views are to be expected in the context of growing student numbers associated with mass higher education.

The majority of students speak incredibly highly of library staff, and describe them as helpful and approachable:

> The library is really good and the service in there is really good as well. If you are stuck with anything there's always leaflets there and people that can help.
>
> Frank, male undergraduate

Specialist services provided within the library are viewed favourably by those who use them, for example, the visual impairment unit. It is recognised that both the institution and the library provide excellent services to students with particular needs:

> Yes it's [the visual impairment unit] quiet, there are only four computers in it and it's specifically for students with visual impairment and we can take as

many books off the shelf as you like and take them in there in peace and quiet. You are handy if you need to speak to anyone at the desk, you're handy to use the Internet, the library catalogues, whatever and you have photocopying facilities there, so it is ideal.

Kerry, female mature student with a visual impairment

Overall, the location of the library within the campus is positively viewed as students feel they can nip in and out of it between classes. Electronic facilities associated with the library, such as the online catalogue and online journals, are favoured by students:

I thought the library was fantastic – there was loads of journal material, loads of books, the library staff were really useful, you could take loans out and renew it on the website which was great cos I stay in Falkirk so it's a problem trying to come into uni to return books and get new books out – being able to renew things on the website is brilliant.

Elizabeth, female undergraduate

It is clear from data collected by the SEP, that students have opinions regarding the library. Students themselves have prioritised the library for discussion in qualitative interviews, giving an indication of how important this service is to them and their experience at GCU. Students relay a diversity of opinions regarding the library, but when critical, are generally understanding of the level of strain placed upon the service by the growing number of students accessing the facility.

These student selected issues, highlighted by the qualitative method, are remarkably consistent with much more structured programmes of evaluation.

Future work for the SEP

The short-term objectives for the SEP are to finalise the longitudinal progression and retention study of cohort 1 as they complete their honours programmes this academic session (2005/06). Members of this group will also be invited to participate in a graduate study, which will attempt to provide an overarching view of their experience and prospects after four years of study at GCU.

Note

1. This case study was contributed by Jim Leahy.

6

Current and recent research in evaluation of library and information services

This chapter reviews practical examples of research into the evaluation of library and information services with a strong focus on practitioner-based research but also including work carried out by research agencies. While research is a minority activity among library and information professionals (McNicol, 2004b) it can at least be said that service evaluation is the commonest activity. There are a number of factors which restrict involvement in research. Communication is often poor between researchers and practitioners, and practitioners can be intimidated by the sophisticated battery of methodologies that professional researchers have at their disposal. Keeping up with the professional literature and current jargon can be difficult. Funding is often lacking to support research, although useful pieces of small-scale research can be done with very little money. Employers might feel that research has little practical application and therefore not worth supporting as a form of staff development. Finally, there is a natural resistance to change and staff who are potentially affected by the research outcomes may be antagonised or feel threatened by the outcomes.

Involvement in research varies from sector to sector with the lowest level of involvement being found among school librarians and the highest in public libraries. Across all the sectors, user surveys is the commonest form of activity. This form of research is notable for being informed by standardised methodologies of the kind described in Chapter 4, such as the CIPFA PLUS methodology and is so well established that it is not even considered to be 'true research'. Involvement in externally funded projects is also common, and a third of academic libraries have been involved in these, such as the JISC funded Big Blue Project on information literacy.

The most common subjects for research in public libraries are: opening hours; the People's Network, which has given a notable fillip to evaluation activities and attracted the attention of professional researchers; lifelong learning; mobile libraries and social inclusion. In health libraries, important areas are journal usage, reflecting the high qualitative level of work in this area; use of interlibrary loans; the information needs of particular groups; and information skills training. These kinds of preoccupations also surface in higher education, although here there has been a major focus on the use of electronic information services, paralleling the interest in the People's Network in public libraries. Because of the smaller amount of activity in school libraries, it is more difficult to identify key issues, although the growth of interest in information literacy is an important factor here. The diverse interests of special libraries also make it difficult to identify issues.

Among the barriers to research are lack of time, a lack of money to fund research and adequate skill levels. One of the most serious problems is that research is only used by those libraries directly involved in it, and is often not more widely recognised or used by others who could benefit from it, which suggests that the principles behind evidence-based information practice are still not widely understood. There is also a need for better communication between academic and practitioner researchers and sharing of good practice.

Some practical examples of library evaluation may be found at two useful, if aging websites: Karen Fischer's *Annotated Bibliography on Library Assessment* (*http://library .ups.edu/kfischer/Bibliography.htm*), last updated December 2003, and BUBL's news survey reports (*http://bubl.ac.uk/ news/surveys/*) last updated in March 2002.

Value and impact

Value and impact have been discussed in general terms in Chapter 2. Studies have been undertaken in several sectors including school, public and higher education libraries.

The impact of the school library resource centre on learning

This study, completed in 2001, described research into the impact of the school library resource centre (Williams and Wavell, 2001) and looked at learning in the broadest sense, including motivation, progression, independence and interaction. The first phase of the study used focus groups and interviews, while the second phase used case studies of particular examples of school library resource centre activity to find out whether this perceived impact was actually taking place. The case studies covered a range of subjects as well as reading for pleasure. The report identified stakeholder groups' perceptions of the wide range of possible learning experiences that might be affected by the school library, the broad range of potential impacts on the learning experience which were observed, examples of indicators of learning, examples of techniques used to monitor the impact of learning and a range of factors which influence the effectiveness of learning in the school library. The study found that librarians had found that 'quality of pupils' learning performance indicators' was a difficult area to address. Indicators therefore had to be heavily linked to curricular goals. The study found that pupils were able to find information relatively easily but had difficulty interpreting and using the information, thus implying an information literacy agenda, a continuing theme in value and impact studies. Schools that integrated resource-based learning into the whole school had less difficulty with this problem. The report importantly noted that 'Teachers and librarians do not yet have a common vision or language to describe the way the school library resource centre interacts with the classroom'. Perhaps because the methodology is essentially qualitative, the report, although data rich, is somewhat lacking in overview conclusions and action points.

Measuring the impact of higher education libraries: The LIRG/SCONUL Impact Implementation Initiative

The LIRG (Library and Information Research Group)/SCONUL (Society of College, National and University Libraries) Impact Implementation Initiative reviewed the impact of higher education libraries on learning, teaching and research and involved 22 participants who attempted to measure the impact of an aspect of their services on their user communities (Payne and Conyers, 2005). This study was motivated by the rapid changes which have permeated higher education and which are blurring the boundaries between libraries, IT student support and academic departments. The effect of technology means that libraries can no longer assume that they have a monopoly over the provision of information to support teaching, learning and research. This is complemented by the growing concern within higher education to seek the views of students about their learning experience as discussed in the previous chapter. The exercise follows on pre-existing instruments, such as the satisfaction surveys described in Chapter 4 and the perceived need to develop a research culture within higher education, making it easier to discover the views of users. An initial review of the situation showed a need to develop standardised methodologies which could be used by all institutions. Of the first ten projects selected, eight were on the theme of information literacy. A fairly complex methodology was developed which involved:

- choosing an area where the library is seeking to measure impact;
- articulating objectives that set out what the library is seeking to achieve in the area chosen;
- developing success criteria by which judgments can be made as to whether those objectives have been met;
- creating impact measures for the chosen area of investigation;
- identifying evidence that needs to be collected;
- selecting appropriate research methods to collect the evidence.

Long-term outputs from the project are likely to include exemplars of impact measurement, guidance on the use of these measures and a toolkit or handbook of research instruments that can be used to gather the evidence.

Shorter-term conclusions from the first ten projects (Blagden, 2005) included a noteworthy predominance of information literacy projects and that information skills are vital but time-consuming to deliver. In addition, the projects on this subject were able to answer management questions about whether the increasing amount of time being devoted to information literacy was well spent and whether generic information literacy resources were as useful as subject specific ones. Many reports mentioned the embedding of information literacy skills further into the curriculum. Increased collaboration with other departments including academic staff was a feature of most projects. The projects also offered an opportunity for participants to develop their research skills, an important issue discussed above. It is hoped it will strengthen the move to evidence-based information practice, although one participant found the exercise more time-consuming than they anticipated and not one they would be able to repeat. A useful further outcome would be the collection of statistics to facilitate impact analysis.

Laser Foundation libraries impact project

This report (Laser Foundation, 2005) was commissioned by the Laser Foundation and carried out by PricewaterhouseCoopers LLP 'in response to the perceived urgent need for the public library sector to be able to demonstrate to local and national government the scale of its contribution to the interests of society'. The general aim was to define and measure in a reproducible way the full impact that libraries have in influencing and supporting their local communities and to ensure that robust data would be available to confirm evidence of impact. The steering group managing the project worked closely with those working on the Department for Culture, Media and Sport (DCMS) Impact Measures and has produced indicators which are complementary but separate from the DCMS measures. The indicators are intended to assist local authorities in developing their impact measures and understanding how they might be best used. Seven public library authorities, mostly notable for their sophisticated approach to performance measurement participated in the study.

The report looked at shared priorities between central and local government and identified four particular priority areas: children, education, health and older people. The report argues that libraries make a clear and measurable contribution to wider policy priorities at both local and national levels. Perhaps, rather obviously, the report emphasises the need to look beyond book borrowing measures. The pilot authorities who contributed both quantitative and qualitative data highlighted a significant contribution to the development of adult skills and child literacy in the education and children shared priority area. The data demonstrated a clear contribution to government objectives on patient and public involvement in health and for older people, the data shows an impact on a range of themes around quality of life and general wellbeing as well as national policy priorities on strengthening independent living. The report identified a number of benefits to developing approaches to impact measures:

- focusing attention on the need to show evidence of how libraries engage with a range of policy areas;

- demonstrating the value of conducting focused research with customers;

- providing powerful data and information to advocate the role of work and libraries;

- linking with cultural change by encouraging a culture of focused evidence gathering by staff;
- supporting planning and service improvement by providing data that can be used to reflect service performance and to make informed decisions about future priorities.

These benefits are, for the most part, already well understood and McNicol's (2004b) comments on the practical difficulties of achieving them are relevant here.

The measures actually chosen are strongly based on existing library activities. For example, two measures have been developed for education:

- The impact on adults by the collection of quantitative data showing the numbers or percentage covered and qualitative data linked to, for example, the impact on confidence and qualifications.
- The impact of libraries on pupils attending summer reading schemes or homework clubs/study support based in libraries by collection and analysis of quantitative data showing the numbers or percentage of participants and qualitative data showing the impact of participants.

Examples of quantitative data to be collected are given and questions listed which support qualitative data collection. Somewhat oddly, the report recommends the use of questionnaires to support qualitative data collection. Examples of qualitative data collection are given, focusing primarily on 'change experiences'.

The report's main recommendation is that a national template of impact measurement should be drawn up, based on the project findings. The report concludes with appendices giving a wealth of detail on methodologies and practical examples which those anxious to pursue work in this area will find invaluable.

What is most notable about this report is its explicit acceptance of government social targets in devising its measures. Nor is it unique in this. Countries as varied as Greece, Portugal and Australia are adopting similar strategies in devising performance indicators. There are two issues here. Should libraries accept government social agendas in devising performance measures, given that governments and their social priorities will change over time, and second, will this encourage public libraries to evolve into social service agencies rather than cultural or educational ones?

Public libraries

Many examples of public library PLUS surveys are available on the Web, some giving shorter reports and some providing detailed results. They usually reflect the structure of the questionnaire. Brighton and Hove City Libraries' summary of the 2004 survey is relatively brief (*http://www.citylibraries .info/information/documents/cipfa_plus_summary_04.doc*).

The report includes some demographic data. Usage by the 20–24 age group is higher than the national average and usage by ethnicity does not exactly match the ethnic demography of Brighton and Hove, suggesting the need to promote increased usage by ethnic minority groups. The increase in first visits to the History Centre and one of the libraries reflects the provision of new or refurbished buildings. While borrowing of books continues to be popular, the use of ICT, borrowing of DVDs and CDs has increased. The library is also being used more for studying, reflecting a growing diversity of use. Success in finding a particular book has declined and a free reservations service is being introduced to help deal with this problem. Views on the physical conditions of the libraries reflected where refurbishments had taken place with users being most appreciative of buildings which had undergone improvements. Satisfaction with opening hours had fallen and this was to be investigated further through community library surveys. Staff helpfulness was highly rated and had even been commended by the Audit Commission. Information and enquiry services and IT services were rated good, although there were mixed views about children's services as space is insufficient in two libraries. Finally, the introduction of a new mobile library will result in the formulation of a new mobile library strategy. The summary is an honest review of strengths and areas for improvement with weaknesses being identified and earmarked for attention.

Redcar and Cleveland Borough Council offer highly detailed analyses linked to the library's objectives and its quality assessment strategy which includes Best Value Review, Charter Mark and Investors in People. The 2001 report (*http://www.redcar-cleveland.gov.uk/YrCouncl.nsf/0/4B4DCBC11F3D637680256C8700540552?OpenDocument*) summarises the library's objectives and achievements.

The library's objectives are:

- to better match services offered in libraries to the needs of library users and potential users;
- to increase the awareness of library services;
- to increase the number of visits made to libraries each year;
- to increase the proportion of citizens of the borough who are members of a library in Redcar and Cleveland.

The fourth objective – to tackle the issue of non-usage is particularly noteworthy. Achievements include the impact of the People's Network which has greatly helped in meeting users' needs, not only for IT services but also to assist in local history, family history and reader development. A leaflet listing library services was produced and sent to every household in the borough and library staff held awareness sessions in local supermarkets and local events. This has resulted in both an increase in the number of library visits and a rise in the number of active borrowers. Comparing the 2001 survey with the one done in 2000 showed that for all key indicators Redcar and Cleveland's results were higher than the UK average. User comments in the free text response box in the questionnaire were complimentary about the service in general and staff in particular. Three areas were, however, identified where satisfaction has fallen and would need to be addressed. These were guiding, opening hours and problems with layout.

A Children's PLUS survey was undertaken in December 2001 which showed a high satisfaction rate with all areas of service, partly due to the refurbishment of some children's libraries. A non-user survey had been undertaken in 2000, which showed that some respondents did not use the libraries as the opening hours were unsuitable. There was also a high level of ignorance about current service provision and a need for better marketing and promotion. A further non-user survey was planned for 2002/03 to determine whether the People's Network had changed the pattern of demand for the hours of access to the library.

Here survey outcomes are clearly being linked to objectives to facilitate a culture of continuous improvement.

Public libraries case study: Norfolk[1]

The county of Norfolk is a large and mainly rural area with a population of just over 800,000 people. Norfolk has 500 communities ranging from Norwich, regional market towns and many small isolated villages and hamlets. Wide economic variations exist. There are wards in the south of the county that are ten times better off than wards in the east of the county. There are areas of great isolation and both urban and rural poverty. There are particular areas of nationally recognised deprivation in Kings Lynn, Great Yarmouth, Thetford and Norwich. The workforce in Norfolk has a low skills base, earnings are less than in other areas of the country, a large number of older people 'retire' to Norfolk and the number of people from ethnic minority backgrounds is small, but significant. Take-up of post-16 learning opportunities in the county is low and this causes worries for the economic sustainability of the county in the future. Literacy and numeracy levels in the county are well below the national average. There are 46 branch libraries in the county, including the Norfolk and Norwich Millennium Library. There is a fleet of 17 mobiles. Additionally, there are the usual libraries in prisons, in hospitals, a housebound service with 7,000 customers and a school library service. There is the usual range of inherited library buildings, most of them too small and many in inconvenient places.

Take-up of library services was not particularly good in the 1990s. The library service had 'lost' a large number of its core users when the old central library burnt down in a fire in 1994; by the year 2000 the situation for libraries in the county was bleak. Just 20 per cent of the population were active members. Visits per head of the population were low and issues were in decline.

If the situation was to be retrieved, then something had to be done about it, and the service simply could not rely on building a big new library to improve usage.

Areas for action identified were:

- More people were needed to use the library service and use it regularly.

- Staff needed to encourage use of all library services, attracting people to both new services and, of course, to continue using established services.

- Income had to be increased and staff needed to start the bandwagon rolling and build up momentum to promote the opening of the Norfolk and Norwich Millennium Library.

To ensure that services were relevant and to a wider community changes had to be made. In marketing services, the community could be divided into four groups:

- those people who are active users (core customers);

- those people who would use the service if they felt they needed to or if it were made it easier for them to use the service – the people who have never quite got around to it;

- those people who don't see a relevance in their lives for libraries;

- finally those people who are frankly hostile to the idea.

The first step was to translate intending users into active users and to start changing the opinions of the indifferent. It would be a waste of effort to spend resources on the hostile group.

It was necessary to understand the whole community and to find out much more about them and what they wanted. This meant market profiling. While the general premise 'libraries are for everyone' applies, within that there are specific segments – but it's not just about demographics, it's about needs, preferences and values.

The following target groups were identified: all required a different marketing message:

- families and children;

- teenagers;

- 25–45-year olds;
- students;
- researchers;
- men;
- full-time workers;
- minority ethnic groups;
- older people;
- lapsed users.

These groups have specific needs and need specific marketing messages. One of the target groups – full-time workers – is discussed below.

Following the destruction of the Norfolk and Norwich central library on 1st August 1994, stakeholders began to think beyond merely replacing the library and considered how to create a much more ambitious project, one where partnership was important and one where the opportunity could be used to develop a library as a blueprint for the twenty-first century, in terms of improved service delivery and to take advantage of technological changes that would enable the library to be more accessible and more responsive to the needs of the people of Norfolk and Norwich. From this evolved the Forum, a vibrant meeting place and the hub of knowledge, information, entertainment and learning opportunities available to the entire region.

The aim of the Millennium Library is to support everyone's reading and learning. It provides an inspirational space that informs the community, supports lifelong learning and encourages a love of reading and knowledge. The new library challenged the traditional view that users had of libraries. People had huge expectations of the place.

So what to do? It wasn't enough to just rely on goodwill to encourage people to begin to use the Norfolk and Norwich Millennium Library, a strategy had to be developed. The strategy can be summed up as:

- a key set of messages;
- defined target audiences;
- very specific promotions;
- consultation and listening;
- community action plans;
- changing the way the service was delivered;
- a robust set of performance indicators and evaluation methods.

It was vital not to offer the same kind of service as before, so staff buy-in was vital. The key messages were focused on reading and learning and inspiration. Staff focused on the benefits of using the service in all service promotions and knew about their communities and had researched their needs. Activities undertaken included a lot of consultation about what people wanted from their library – focusing on the pre-identified target groups. Community action plans are part of the community profiling process and associated planning process. The results of consultation meant that staff changed stock profiles to match the target audiences – so now Norfolk libraries no longer solely satisfy a particular type of customer.

It was important to get the right books and sound and vision materials on the shelves, and it was particularly important to change the way the service was delivered. This meant taking into account the needs and demands of customers that the library is open at convenient hours, with staff to help customers find information, rather than put barriers in their way, all in an environment that puts customers at their ease. Library users now are at the heart of the service offered and this has accompanied the development of the library with a staff development programme that supports the change in service delivery. Changing the culture of the library is something that is easy to say, but not always easy to implement, but it is essential if libraries are to remain relevant to communities in the twenty-first century. The customer focus programme that all staff have attended demonstrated how an individual's behaviour can affect customers. Staff have been empowered to keep library customers by relaxing rules and enabling them to respond better to individual customer needs. Finally, the staff demographic profile is being changed – employing more young people, more men and more people from ethnic minority backgrounds, all with a very strong service ethos.

Promoting the service to full-time workers

One of the target groups for the Millennium Library was full-time workers. Norwich has a large travel to work catchment area, with a great many service industries based in the city centre – major employers in the city are Norwich Union and the city council.

Staff wanted to highlight the benefits of using the library to workers in the city, so they developed a plan to increase membership and use over the lunch period. At the outset, staffing was reviewed so that when more people started using the service, they were not put off by having to wait in long queues due to a lack of staff. There are self-service machines in the Millennium Library, as well as high-interest, popular contemporary fiction and non-fiction attractively displayed on the ground floor in a section called 'Express'. A series of lunchtime reading groups in the library were also set up. Finally, to the horror of many staff who had been working for the library service for years and years, the rules about eating and drinking in the library were relaxed. This had a beneficial effect on the lives of library floorwalkers who had been spending time telling people that eating and drinking wasn't allowed in the library. This had no harmful effects.

Articles were placed in the house magazines of the city council and Norwich Union, selling the benefits of using the Millennium Library, with an application form and a free DVD/video loan voucher. Staff emphasised that it was cheaper to borrow books than to buy them, that it was quick and convenient to use and also emphasised that to borrow films and music from the library was cheaper and more convenient due to longer loan periods. Because people don't necessarily live in Norwich, they were told that they could borrow their books from the Millennium Library and return them at any other branch. This was evaluated simply by counting the number of free video vouchers exchanged and how many people joined using the application form.

Norwich city centre has lots of other employers, so the expertise of staff in the business library who used marketing databases was utilised to identify places in the city that employed more than ten staff and where they were likely to have a staff room. They were sent a poster, application forms with free loan vouchers and a load of flyers. Again, evaluation was simple, and the response from both approaches was amazing.

Evaluation of the marketing process was done as follows:

- Focus groups. This allowed staff to explore the impact that libraries are having on individual lives and the life of the community. In the past year focus groups have carried out with blind and visually impaired people, older people, young men, 'looked after' children (refugees and asylum seekers under 18) and young people in general. A focus group of young people helped design the children's library.

- Mystery shopping. Many libraries are mystery shopped to see whether they are giving the right information. At the Millennium Library customer service is evaluated using shoppers from the target groups. The results are used to improve practices.

- Two sets of market research have been commissioned on the library experience for new members. One was the baseline, the other following an action plan measured any effects that the work had had. This was done as a telephone survey. Another piece of commissioned research was something similar for lapsed users, people who joined but hadn't used the services for a year. The results of this showed that in the main, people stop using the service because something changes in their lives, they change job, they move house and the library habit is something that got left behind.

- It has been made easier for customers to reach staff with comments and suggestions about the service. Analysis of these is carried out and everyone receives a reply. Examples of the things which were changed in response to comments and suggestions include opening the library on bank holiday Saturdays and opening the children's library on Sunday, for both of which staff were able to use the comments to support a bid for extra revenue. Another example was about the classification system used in the library. When the library was opened, there was a subject library layout which meant that people who were trying to apply a numerical logic to finding their way around the stock became quickly unstuck.

- An annual PLUS survey. But staff also survey when they want to change newspaper subscriptions, for example, or asking young people about categorisation of teenage fiction.

- Linked to the social exclusion policy and to the target groups, such as ethnic minorities, parents, non-users (men and teenagers mainly), people with learning disabilities, people with disabilities, staff regularly invite people from these groups to come and talk to senior staff meetings. This is good from two points of view. First, staff get to know what barriers people face in accessing the services, what they like and dislike about the service, and what it would take to make them switch from being an intender to an active user. Second, it shows the trust that staff have built up with target communities, in that they are willing to come and talk to the library.

- Target groups are involved in developing the libraries: young people help staff select materials for the library, people from ethnic minority groups help to select books and sound and vision items, when people tell staff that the stock is poor in certain areas, a team librarian will ring them up and ask them how it can be improved. Most recently target groups have begun to be involved in the staff selection process. This has been used this in the selection of development workers for teenagers and early-years literacy.

- A lot of in-library research is carried out. The look and feel of a place is vital in marketing services effectively. Staff notice how people are using the space and make decisions about the location of services using this information.

Staff also use the aspiring to inclusion framework developed by Suffolk County Council to improve services – this is a framework in which priority groups are identified and involved in an action planning process. It uses both surveys and focus groups. Increasingly the Museums, Libraries and Archives Council's Generic Learning Outcomes are used in the evaluation of activities. As well as evaluations of specific promotions, follow-ups are undertaken with individuals, particularly those people from priority groups who joined the library as part of a specific piece of work.

Measuring outcomes

- Issues are increasing and now that the Millennium Library has been open for three years the effect of the halo should have been diminished.

- Visitor figures are very healthy. During half-term week in 2004, staff welcomed 31,572 people to the library, the highest number ever.

- This story is reflected across the county – this is a library service that is responsive and reflects customer needs and preferences. Market penetration has increased. In the year 2000, 20 per cent of the local population were active users and this has now risen to 27 per cent.

Conclusions

The Norfolk and Norwich Millennium Library has been successful in targeting its core markets to make visiting the library and borrowing books part of the lifestyle of a wider group of customers. Staff at the library are aware that different user groups need different marketing approaches, and that marketing the library is not simply about advertising but is about total service delivery.

Special libraries case study: Pfizer Ltd[2]

Background

The Walton Oaks Information Centre at Pfizer was created in 2002, developed from a centralisation of departmental information stores.

Pfizer is a research-based global pharmaceutical company, and the Walton Oaks Information Centre sits within the part of the business that markets leading prescription and consumer medicines for humans and animals.

The librarian's information experience has principally been within corporate pharmaceutical environments.

The Information Centre team of four provides a service for all staff (around 800) based at the Walton Oaks site. Its purpose is to proactively support key user groups across the business with direct access to essential, high-quality information. It is a centre of excellence for advice and expertise in the provision of information, training and consultancy on information science and management.

This case study illustrates how the Information Centre team has used evaluation to measure progress achieved, and developed a culture of continuous improvement.

Measurable opportunities

Since its launch in 2002, the team has used selected opportunities to measure success:

- launch event;
- birthday events/participation at company street fairs;
- creating team standards;
- revising role profiles.

Each event has a specific set of objectives attached to it, for example, increasing user visits or number of visitors to the birthday stand; these are measured both before and after the event to determine the effectiveness of the event itself and the impact on user behaviours. Team standards ensure new and existing team members are clear on key processes, focused on the user needs and the services provided. New role profiles for team members were developed to support the standards and ensure clarity of day-to-day accountabilities and behaviours required for the Information Centre.

Gathering data

Usage statistics have been gathered, and refined annually. The team has created tools to record and measure user behaviours effectively. These include an Access database for recording user enquiries and their usage of the quiet areas; a library management system used for cataloguing, lending and interlibrary loans that produces useful reports, and mechanisms for collecting user feedback.

User feedback is gathered in a number of ways:

- informally by collecting spontaneous compliments in a central e-mail folder;
- formally through annual user surveys;
- seeking out feedback when contributing to specific business projects;
- using the cross-functional user group that acts as an advisory board and provides two-way feedback to and from their departments.

The feedback is then utilised in different manners:

- some is followed up for more value-added information and crafted into short case studies, which are used in posters or panels for future events;
- others are developed into articles and published in in-house magazines.

The key factor is to use the corporate language to ensure anyone in the business can understand the message(s) the Information Centre is trying to convey. One of the most powerful ways of communicating success is to let users express benefits to others, and the user group has been invaluable in doing this on a routine basis.

Continuous improvement

It is not sufficient to simply set measures and gather data or feedback from users. The team has strived to refine and improve upon each and every measure, reviewing them after each event and also annually.

From a review of the first year's usage figures, the team developed additional fields in the Access database to log requests by product, department and time spent on the request. This enables monthly reports to senior managers to be presented as colourful and meaningful graphs with links to organisational events, such as strategic planning that create natural peaks in information requests. The team has been able to see that the Pfizer performance management cycle, particularly at personal development plan time, also affects requests.

Performance indicators continue to be refined to ensure the team is measuring not just usage numbers, but also areas of added value to the organisation, such as time saved for a business project.

The team conducts a formal annual review of activities, which is summarised in a 'year in review' document. This is a mixture of key usage information with trends and highlights. It has very few words and many pictures or graphs. It is written in the corporate language and each item is included only if it demonstrates value added by the team to the business. The year in review serves two purposes: one for the team in understanding what went well the previous year and what it might do differently the next. Second, it is distributed to directors of the users' groups to inform them of the role the Information Centre has had with their departments during the year.

These activities, including the promotional events, have resulted in spontaneous feedback from the current finance director: 'The Information Centre provides an invaluable service that is vital for our company'. In practical terms, it has meant that the Information Centre has been the only information group to have grown in spatial size following the merger with Pharmacia in 2003.

Finally, user surveys have evolved significantly over the three years from quite detailed service feedback to focusing on obtaining benefits and impact of the service on users' daily work.

The approach

Now that there are a number of years' usage information and year in review documents, this information is being used in other ways. One such new way is to predict future usage trends and associated requirements in resources. The team is able to look at new product launches and estimate the knock-on effect in resource usage. The information has also been applied to extend use of the services beyond the prescription-only medicine side of the business, and now includes consumer health and field-based colleagues. It has also resulted in a new corporately-based funding model.

Overall, the Pfizer Walton Oaks Information Centre team's approach is to have a combined qualitative and quantitative focus. The Pfizer organisation talks in numbers, so it is important for the Information Centre team to use metrics that the rest of the business will understand. It is critical that the Information Centre talks in the same language as the rest of the organisation, for example, not many people understand document delivery, but when this is translated into scientific articles to support your marketing process, then users are much clearer.

The team has worked hard to communicate the results of their measures, so there is little point in keeping all this useful information for themselves. Let stakeholders know what the team is achieving to secure longer-term resourcing and continued success of the service. Communicating this is as important as the evaluation itself.

Finally, it is imperative to act on the information that is gathered. The team has changed services, cutting some back, starting new ones or improving on the 2004 user survey to build on what was learnt in the 2003 survey.

Conclusions

- In order to not just survive, but also thrive, an information centre must be aligned and linked to business goals (both local and regional) not the other way around.

- Every opportunity should be taken to gather meaningful data for evaluating service provision, then put into context and communicated across the user population.

- Reflecting on how far the team has come and looking forward to where it is going are vital for gaining confidence, not only from the team, but also from important stakeholders.

- Continuously setting, refining and learning from using tools for evaluation is critical for understanding the user population and the level(s) of service required.

After all, a business like Pfizer does not stand still and neither should the information centre that serves it.

Some examples from Poland

The Maria Konopnicka Public Library

Since 1989, Polish librarians in all types of library have worked hard to develop a service appropriate to the needs of a modern democratic society and this includes the evaluation of the services they are developing. The results reflect this process of development as studies of a public library service and an academic library show.

The study of the Maria Konopnicka Public Library in Suwalki (Nowacka, 2002) was motivated by the need to analyse local community needs using a more social science-based approach than the previous method of informally observing patterns of family life. Another factor is the need to make a case for improved funding in a time of increased competition for resources. The disappearance of censorship after 1989 meant that it was necessary to develop a more liberal approach to stock building. The pre-existing stock had a general literary content and contact with both teachers and schoolchildren showed that older pupils wanted textbooks on economics and law to help them pass university entrance exams. Users were also becoming aware of the existence of expensively produced titles with high-quality colour illustrations which the library was quite unable to afford. An analysis of library statistics for 1999 showed that while the number of users was increasing, the number of loans was declining and there were insufficient funds to purchase new titles. As there was no hope that the acquisitions budget would grow substantially, the only way forward was to identify user needs as precisely as possible and try to satisfy them. Fortunately there was a large amount of statistical data to go on. This showed that over half the library's users were schoolchildren and over 15 per cent of the library's users were future students. Occupationally, the most distinguishing feature was the virtual disappearance of the farming class who had once made up over 60 per cent of users. Priority was therefore given to younger users and a questionnaire was devised to identity their needs more precisely. This showed, perhaps, not surprisingly that the main preference was for current best-sellers, such as *Bridget Jones' Diary*. To encourage book use, Polish authors are regularly asked to visit the library to talk about their work. A course of lectures, given by academics, was also organised for local schoolchildren on the theme of how to become a student.

A key stakeholder group has therefore been identified and its needs recognised and publicised through outreach activities. Good cooperation has also been achieved with schools and it is planned to extend this approach to other stakeholder groups, such as office workers and the unemployed.

A study of four Polish academic libraries

This survey was undertaken using the Libra software package produced by Priority Search UK (Buzdygan et al., 2000).

This was done primarily to identify user needs and produce a comparative analysis of the four participants. The users were asked to answer the question, how can the library service be improved? The questionnaire consisted of three parts: a demographic section, a rating scale section and a paired comparison section. The respondents had to identify their priorities from paired comparisons. This produced four top priorities which were: more books (all libraries), more periodicals (three libraries), more computers for Internet use (three libraries), and multiple copy provision of textbooks (three libraries). These findings are pretty much the common coin of academic library evaluation, although opening hours does not feature in the top four issues.

Notes

1. This case study was contributed by Jan Holden.
2. This case study was contributed by Sophie Graham.

7

The evaluation of electronic information services

Although the evaluation of electronic information services has been going on for ten years or more, it still warrants a separate chapter of its own. Electronic performance issues have certainly found their way into general survey instruments, such as the SCONUL template, the LibQUAL+™ instrument and the public libraries PLUS surveys. However, the traditional/print environment and the electronic environment differ dramatically in important key areas, such as information seeking behaviour and the ability of users to engage and extract content. Lumping together traditional and networked services leads to confused data and results, and potentially erroneous conclusions regarding customer perceptions of outcomes and service quality. It is also likely that users may provide feedback about a 'library service' which is not actually provided by the library, such as leased online databases (Bertot, 2004).

It was early recognised that electronic information services had radically altered the concept of a library. Library services were traditionally provided in a building, providing materials owned by the library to physical visitors during opening hours. The coming of the electronic library changed all that. Libraries provided a service available through a network which made it more difficult for users to grasp the simple fact that they were using library services at all. Visitors became 'virtual' because they could use the service whenever they wanted and were not constrained by library opening hours. This led to the use of terms like the electronic library, the virtual library and the digital library. In reality, libraries had become hybrids offering a mixture of traditional print and also electronic services. The situation is naturally confusing to users who use electronic library services along with other networked services and who may not be able to distinguish between electronic information databases of the traditional kind and websites of all kinds. thus providing a problem for those trying to evaluate the use of electronic information services.

Not surprisingly, early work focused on definitions and clearly defined indicators. The Equinox Project (*http://equinox.dcu.ie/*) defined a library collection as 'All information resources provided by a library for its users. Comprises resources held locally and remote resources for which access has been acquired, at least for a certain period of time.' The electronic library was further defined as 'The electronic documents and databases the library service decides to make available in its collections, plus the library OPAC (catalogue) and home page'. Equinox provided a draft list of 14 performance indicators some of which have been widely adopted, such as 'number of logins to the electronic library service', 'number of remote logins to the electronic library service' and library computer workstation use rate. 'Number of remote logins' has spawned other indicators because there is naturally interest in where this activity is taking place. Initially, this was mainly the home, but the workplace is becoming increasingly important, with implications for educational developments, such as work-based learning and the use of information literacy in the workplace. Interestingly enough, length of session was not included. The evaluation culture implied was essentially one of counting and was partly due to the fact that electronic information databases are often passworded and consequently usage statistics were easy to collect. Qualitative issues were not really addressed other than suggesting user satisfaction surveys.

Indicators have been further refined for different purposes. The revised ISO 2789 (Sumsion, 2002) identifies four core datasets as priority items:

- number of sessions;
- number of documents downloaded;
- number of records downloaded;
- number of virtual visits (from outside the library).

There are also four additional indicators to be collected where appropriate:

- session time;
- number of rejected sessions (turns away);
- number of searches (queries);
- number of Internet sessions.

It was also considered desirable to count separately:

- provision inside the library;
- provision outside the library premises but inside the parent institution;
- outside the parent institution.

In reality, it can be difficult to identify the second indicator 'provision outside the library premises, but inside the parent institution' separately. The use of conventional survey techniques was also recommended and the revision points to typical questions which can be asked about user activity in the electronic domain.

The E-Measures Project which piloted e-measures with several UK academic libraries (*http://www.ebase.uce.ac.uk/emeasures/emeasures.htm*) includes a repertoire of indicators more appropriate to higher education. These include:

- number of unique electronic full-text serials received by subscription;
- number of electronic databases received by subscription;
- number of e-books purchased or licensed;
- number of successful requests for full-text articles.

Counting sessions of various types measures only volume of activity and does not address the deceptively simple question, what is going on? What meaningful use is being made of the services accessed and, crucially, what impact are they having on users?

Studies in this area go back to the mid-1990s and relate mainly to higher education. Oliver Obst's (1995) study of Internet use by students at Muenster University is a useful pioneering example. These studies were undertaken by academic librarians to evaluate the use being made of the important new services they were providing, and the initial results were not encouraging.

The first cycle of the Justeis Project, one of the first major studies of the use of electronic information services (EIS) by students, found the resources most used by students to be the Internet, OPACs and e-mail. The use of e-journals, web databases and JISC mediated services was also found to be low (Armstrong, 2001). Another major longitudinal study is the Jubilee Project (*http://online.northumbria.ac.uk/faculties/art/information_studies/imri/rarea/im/hfe/jub/hfjubilee.htm*) which examined a range of subject areas and initially identified little change in patterns of usage over time.

The Jubilee Project described a repertoire of issues which are finding their way into EIS evaluation:

- insufficient number of PCs for student access;
- insufficient number of high-spec machines for staff use;
- usage statistics from publishers of limited value;
- extent of integration of EIS into the curriculum;
- problems with password notification;
- multiplicity of passwords;
- access to and reliability of printing facilities;
- ICT skills in relation to age of user;
- off-site access restrictions;
- insufficient technical support;
- disciplines at different evolutionary stages;
- effects of mode of attendance;
- users' ability to evaluate quality of EIS.

The Jubilee cycle (3)[1] reported, inter alia, that nearly two-thirds of those questioned said they had access to a networked PC at home. The majority of students perceived themselves to be at an intermediate skill level in using EIS. There was concern, that for large numbers of students, those using the Internet appeared to possess little awareness of the need to evaluate information found via the Web. Two-thirds of the student questionnaire respondents claimed to have come to depend on EIS in their role as students. Across the six sites surveyed, the level of general student use of EIS was seen as extremely disparate.

Other recent studies provide some comparative data. Baruchson-Arbib and Shor's (2002) study of Israeli college students found that the main use was the Internet. Those with prior experience of computers used EIS significantly more than those who without experience, a finding replicated in other studies. Students who were encouraged by lecturers used EIS more than those who were not encouraged by lecturers. The researchers noted that students may not know or distinguish between different EIS resources, a finding which other studies strongly corroborate. Seamans' (2002) study focused primarily on first-year students' perceptions of information literacy but also gathered data on Internet use which was found to be heavy due to encouragement given by high school teachers. All the students reported little use of indexes and abstracts which they found difficult to use. An American study of first-year students (Waldman, 2003) showed that 94 per cent of students had access to a computer at home; 73 per cent reported using the Internet daily. Data on actual usage showed Lexis/Nexis to be the most used service (44 per cent of respondents), followed by the library catalogue (36 per cent); 50 per cent reported using electronic resources from home. Sixty-seven per cent reported that they found most information for their papers through the Internet, while only 27 per cent reported using EIS. Age and gender were not found to be issues.

In an unpublished survey, Andrew Hewitson (2002) found, in researching the behaviour of students at Leeds Metropolitan University that, in the majority of cases, there was a direct link between the use of EIS and perceived IT competency. Those with advanced IT application and web browser skills were more likely to use EIS. Those who were beginners were more likely to consult traditional library sources.

Although the Internet was the EIS resource most heavily used by students, there appeared to be a low take-up of subscription-based services. These services are particularly important in providing students with an opportunity to keep up to date in their subject area. However, the survey highlights that many of these services, such as electronic indexes and abstracts and electronic journals, were not used frequently by students. This would suggest that many students are not fully aware of the different EIS that are available to support their subject area.

There were concerns that students were bypassing Leeds Metropolitan University's learning centre's web pages and going to information via search engines. As a result, they were missing out on many of the services that are only available via the learning centre's web pages. Although it was only briefly touched on in this research, there is an issue concerning student awareness of EIS prior to entering university, with many acknowledging as to having no previous experience prior to university.

In a study of students at Glasgow Caledonian University, Crawford et al. (2004) found that there was a hierarchy of usage of EIS by subject with paramedicine at the top, business school subject areas in the middle and science and technology at the bottom. Subject was, therefore, the main determinant of EIS use, followed by integration into the programme. Part-time and non-traditional students were more likely to be registered with Athens than full-time students, with the consequence that off-campus use was growing and was segmenting into different components with a growing emphasis on workplace access. The link between IT skills and the intensity of EIS usage was found to be in decline, an indication presumably that IT skills have now reached the level where they are less of an issue. Gateways and links were little used and the catalogue was found to have sunk to third place as the preferred method of accessing EIS. There was a clear link between EIS usage and student progression and retention. Students in subject areas with a good progression rate through the levels and who completed their programmes were also likely to be the heaviest users of EIS. The converse was also found to be the case. There was also a link between EIS usage and innovative learning and teaching methods. Students studying in subject areas where innovative learning and teaching methods were used were also found to be heavier users of EIS than those studying in subject areas where more traditional methods were employed. EIS usage was therefore found to be indissolubly linked to the teaching and learning process as a whole. A follow-up study (Crawford, 2006) reviewed the link between EIS usage and information literacy by administering questionnaires to both current students and alumni. An electronic questionnaire was administered to current students and a traditional paper questionnaire was sent to alumni using the university's alumni database as a sampling frame. The outcomes from both questionnaires were used to create a longitudinal picture and establish key indicators. It was found that respondents broadly understood the concept of information literacy, although this was much more marked among alumni as a result of the experience of work. The relationship of work activity to information literacy was found to be central, and alumni felt that an understanding of information literacy gave them a distinct advantage in job finding and seeking promotion. Unemployed alumni are correspondingly disadvantaged. In many cases information seeking skills, learned at university, could be directly applied to the workplace and scholarly methods were found to be spreading there, although the attitude of employers was variable.

The Jubilee fifth annual report (2004), reviewing a longitudinal study covering five years found some cause for optimism. Higher education was found to be making greater progress towards seamless delivery than further education, but progression had been largely due to trial and error over time. Student usage of electronic information services had increased from 40 per cent to nearly 80 per cent of students between 1999 and 2004. This improvement was related to ease of access but it was also noted that most students do not evaluate the information they receive electronically. Licensing and authentication procedures need to be streamlined. Academic staff continue to be the single greatest influence in student choice of appropriate resources. The report also noted 'assessment of information skills is essential and needs to be recognised as an implicit part of student learning but made explicit in programme assessment'.

'E-measurement' is not without its critics. Town (2004b) who has criticised the 'size and numbers element' of library performance measurement has pointed to 'the inability to see the complex truths beyond the figures'. Factors which need to be taken into account include the flow of electronic information, information literacy skills and their measurement, and satisfaction and experience measures. A balanced scorecard of e-measures is proposed which includes five perspectives: financial, customer, process (delivery), staff development and organisational learning and development.

In the wider world of general and public library usage, the People's Network has been a major fillip to evaluation. In evaluating the People's Network in the north-east of England, Gannon-Leary et al. (2003) found that over two-thirds of users were using the People's Network to search for a specific subject on the Internet. Other uses included e-mailing, word processing and shopping on the Internet. The People's Network was principally used for pleasure but other uses included independent learning and following a course of study. The main reason for using the People's Network was lack of computing facilities at home, because the service was free, and because of the software available. Usage was quite heavy with nearly half of respondents reporting using the People's Network two to three times a week and most respondents (82 per cent) found the People's Network PCs very useful. Only 3 per cent had suggestions for improvements. Reported skill levels followed a fairly conventional pattern with 57 per cent believing their IT skills to be intermediate and only 16 per cent believing that they had advanced IT skills. Looking to the future, library staff training and development was seen to be the key issue.

The People's Network has inspired the Longitude Toolkit (*http://www.mla.gov.uk/action/pn/longitude.asp*), a major evaluation project produced by the Centre for Research in Library and Information Management for The Museums, Libraries and Archives Council. The aim of the toolkit is to enable public libraries to assess the impact over time of end-user electronic services provided in the library, both on individuals and on the community. By checking impact over time, it is intended to assess change, and to check whether original impacts are being sustained. The toolkit is for public library managers seeking to gather reliable information on the overall impact of their services, within local, regional and national contexts, and to demonstrate and exemplify significant impacts on individuals. The toolkit was the outcome of two data collection exercises (Craven and Brophy, 2004) and unlike early evaluation strategies concentrates on qualitative approaches which illuminate more readily available quantitative data. Qualitative data collected during the project covered such information needs as learning a new skill, helping to find work, local history and community information, and shopping and finance, an indication of the kind of information sought via the Internet in a public library setting. The toolkit covers planning longitudinal impact assessment and data collection techniques including interviews, focus groups, diaries and observation. Sampling methods, data analysis and data use and presentation are also covered. An attractive feature of the toolkit is that it can also be usefully consulted by those undertaking survey and evaluation work of a more general nature.

MORI (2005) has produced a major survey *Understanding the Audience* (*http://www.common-info.org.uk/mori-findings .shtml*) which was the first to take a wide ranging look at the issues of reliability of information found on the Internet and the extent to which users feel they can trust the information they find there. Issues like usage and expertise were also reviewed. Over half of the respondents were found to be Internet users. Better-off people (social classes ABC1), those who are under 55 and those with formal qualifications and in work were more likely to use the Internet, while poorer people (social classes C2DE) over 55 with no formal qualifications were less likely to use the Internet. Lapsed Internet users tend to be young people, educated at least to GCSE level and in work. This might be because the conclusion of education and training reduces the need to use the Internet. However, other research shows that that the experience of work encourages the continuation of Internet use. People who have never used the Internet are likely to be older, to have no formal educational qualifications and be unemployed. Home is the most common place of access (80 per cent of respondents). Over half of all respondents (53 per cent) use the Internet at least once a week, less heavy usage than the People's Network, apparently. Although over half of Internet users (60 per cent) have been using it for four years or more, only 10 per cent have received any formal training in how to use the Internet but the majority feel that they do not need any additional help.

The main barrier to using the Internet is lack of interest, lack of convenient access and cost. Non-users do have subject interests which point a way forward, for example, local information, historical information and genealogical research. As with the People's Network study, searching for specific information in connection with a recreational activity is the main reason for use, hobbies and booking flights being two examples. For searching websites, search engines are naturally preferred, with over 80 per cent using this method. Over three-quarters of respondents do not find using the Internet difficult. For half of the respondents the Internet is now their first port of call for finding information and their preferred information source.

For librarians, the authority of the source has always been a key issue and reliability of content of websites is a key factor for respondents as well as quality and up-to-dateness of content. In judging the quality of websites, the trustworthiness of the providing organisation is an important factor. Respondents were more likely to trust museums and libraries than commercial organisations like utility companies, travel agencies and Internet-only retail companies.

This brief survey shows the need to concentrate on patterns of activity as well as number counting and link the evaluation of the usage of electronic information services to the wider world of people's lives and how they interact with electronic resources in both their working and private lives.

Note

1. More information about the project is available from the website: *http://online.northumbria.ac.uk/faculties/art/ information_studies/imri/rarea/im/hfe/jub/hfjubilee.htm* (last accessed: 6 January 2006).

8

The challenge of information literacy and an afterword

An underlying theme throughout this book has been the growing importance of information literacy, which is defined as 'knowing when and why you need information, where to find it, and how to evaluate it, use and communicate it in an ethical manner'. Williams and Wavell (2001) found that pupils were able to find information relatively easily but had difficulty interpreting and using the information they had found. The Jubilee Fifth and Final Annual Report (2004) found that most students did not evaluate the information they received electronically and assessment of information skills is essential. Crawford (2006) highlighted the importance of information literacy in the workplace because of its key contribution to decision making, professional success and contribution to promotion. The MORI (2005) survey found that fewer than 10 per cent of respondents had received formal training on how to use the Internet. As indicated in Chapter 2, information literacy is linked to lifelong learning and social inclusion because it potentially links all types of library including school, university and public and encourages the development of skills which can be carried over into the world of work. It has life-changing potential and can even be viewed as a civil right. Andretta (2005: 57–8) has emphasised that information literacy is indeed a lifelong learning culture. She argues that 'passive' (taught) learning is outdated and inadequate to address the challenges of developing lifelong learning competencies. She calls for a 'constructivist' approach which fosters a student centred perspective within a learning environment characterised by problem-solving activities. The focus is shifting from 'what one learns [to] how one learns'. The emphasis is therefore on the development of transferable skills rather than on the accomplishment of specific tasks. Information literacy should be promoted 'as a vehicle of enhancing critical enquiry and self-directed learning as a foundational element of a broader focus on lifelong learning'.

There is clearly a major challenge to evaluation here. The evaluation of library and information services began in the pre-Internet era and basically focused on what users did in libraries. The Internet and the distribution of electronic information took us further afield, initially into the home and now into the workplace. Evaluation of the usage of electronic information services has made us look much more closely at how information is used, how it impacts on all aspects of peoples' lives and how it changes them. It is no longer just what they do when they are in the library. It is now necessary to engage much more closely with learning and educational processes, and new skills are needed by the evaluator of information services. Indeed, the word *library* seems much less important in this new world.

This links too, to the increasingly social orientation of the process of evaluation. Over 40 years ago Groombridge noted:

> ...those librarians who believe some sociological understanding of the people in their areas to be an essential complement to their professional skills, are

surely those likely to advance the service to new levels of public relevance and successful provision. (Groombridge, 1964: 90)

These words have proven prophetic. Public library PLUS surveys and the SCONUL template now include questions about gender, ethnicity and disability, and while comprehensive university evaluation programmes like that at the University of Central England do not collect comprehensive information about library services, they do at least point librarians in higher education to the need to collect social information. The Laser Foundation (2005) report explicitly links public libraries to government priority areas in the fields of children, education, health and older people thus linking libraries to social policy, an approach which is found in other parts of Europe and indeed in other parts of the world. This widening of objectives and the spreading use of the Internet by people of the most varied backgrounds necessarily also widens what constitutes an information need. In the era of Savage and Groombridge this meant 'the supply of books', but the avalanche of new media and electronic sources of information have changed all that. Examples of information activity quoted in previous chapters include booking a cheap flight, participating in summer reading schemes, providing pharmaceutical information and even encouraging users from ethnic minorities to participate in book selection. Impact studies are already helping to assess how people use this complex information world and what changes it makes to their lives. The world of work seems to offer fruitful prospects for the future. Recent research shows how information literacy is applied to all aspects of work: searching recruitment websites to find job opportunities; finding out about potential employers and what kind of skills they are looking for in recruits; preparing job applications and CV design; finding information to support decision making and keep up to date with new developments; facilitating continuing professional development; and supporting moves towards promotion. More work is needed, too, on how the school leaver can develop and use information literacy skills. The UK Government's report, *Skills, Getting on in Business, Getting on at Work*, emphasises the need for a skilled workforce and although only ICT skills are specifically mentioned, there is a clear need for information literacy skills to be promoted within this context. The report notes:

> Skills are fundamental to achieving our ambitions, as individuals, for our families and for our communities. They help businesses create wealth, and the help people realise their potential. So they serve the twin goals of social justice and economic success. (Department for Education and Skills, 2005; vol. 1: 1)

In public libraries it was envisaged that the introduction of Best Value would result in the introduction of quality officers in public libraries (Crawford 2000: 120). To some extent this has happened. The London Borough of Sutton has a Quality Services Manager and similar posts exist in other parts of London. In most types of library, quality management is often combined with other activities and it will be interesting to see if this pattern changes in future years.

Evaluation has travelled a long way from the Spartan world of single-sided A4 questionnaires to the rich and complex world of today with its wide range of methods. There is no reason to believe that this world will become simpler in the future, and new methods of enquiry may still be needed.

Appendix A
The SCONUL template 2005

The SCONUL questionnaire is published by kind permission of SCONUL (Society of College, National and University Libraries).

Library satisfaction survey

Please help us further improve library and information services by taking a few minutes to complete this short questionnaire.

Please complete *all* questions apart from the last (Question 14 – any other comments and suggestions), which is optional.

About you

1. **Which group are you in?**

   Undergraduate ☐

   Postgraduate (Taught Course) ☐

   Postgraduate (Research) ☐

   Academic Staff ☐

   Other Staff ☐

   Other ☐

2. Are you:

Full-Time	☐
Part-Time	☐
Not Applicable	☐

3. Which Faculty/School/Department are you in:

A	☐
B	☐
C	☐
D	☐
Not Applicable	☐

4. What is your age group:

21 years and under	☐
22 – 26 years	☐
27 – 39 years	☐
40 – 49 years	☐
50 and over	☐

5. Are you:

Female	☐
Male	☐

6. What is your ethnic group?

Ethnic monitoring helps to ensure that our services are relevant to the needs of all ethnic groups and are provided fairly. We therefore invite you to assist us by answering the following question. This is in accordance with best practice as advised by the Commission for Racial Equality, and our statutory duty under the Race Relations Act 2000.

Please choose *one* group to indicate your cultural background.

Asian or British Asian: Indian	☐
Asian or British Asian: Pakistani	☐
Asian or British Asian: Bangladeshi	☐
Asian or British Asian: Chinese	☐
Asian or British Asian: Any Other Asian Background	☐
Black or Black British: Caribbean	☐
Black or Black British: African	☐
Black or Black British: Any Other Black Background	☐
Mixed: White and Black Caribbean	☐
Mixed: White and Black African	☐
Mixed: White and Asian	☐
Mixed: Any Other Mixed Background	☐
White: British	☐
White: Irish	☐
White: Any Other Background	☐

If you selected 'Any Other ... Background' please complete the box below

```
┌──────────────────────────────────────────────┐
│                                              │
│                                              │
│                                              │
│                                              │
└──────────────────────────────────────────────┘
```

Your use of library and information services

7. **Which branch of the Library do you use most frequently?**

Main Library/Learning Resources Centre	☐
Branch A	☐

Branch B ☐

Branch C ☐

Branch D ☐

Branch E ☐

Not applicable ☐

8. **On average, how frequently do you visit that library?**

Several times a day ☐

Once a day ☐

Several times a week ☐

Once a week ☐

Less than once a week ☐

Less than once a month ☐

9. **On average, how often do you access library and information services via a computer (e.g. the library catalogue, e-journals, electronic resources like Web of Knowledge, &c)?**

Several times a day ☐

Once a day ☐

Several times a week ☐

Once a week ☐

Less than once a week ☐

Less than once a month ☐

10. **Please think about the various activities you did the last time you visited the library _in person_. How successful were you in completing these?**

	Very successful	Fairly successful	Neither successful nor unsuccessful	Fairly unsuccessful	Very unsuccessful	Don't know or Not applicable
Looked for library materials on the shelves						
Sought help from library staff						
Borrowed library materials						
Used a PC in the library						

11. Please think about the various activities you did the last time you accessed library and information services via a computer. How successful were you in completing these?

	Very successful	Fairly successful	Neither successful nor unsuccessful	Fairly unsuccessful	Very unsuccessful	Don't know or Not applicable
Used the library catalogue						
Made a reservation on the library system						
Renewed a loan on the library system						
Used an electronic journal						
Used an electronic resource (eg Web of Knowledge)						

12. We'd like you to rate your satisfaction with the following library services, along with how important you think they are:

	Very satisfied	Fairly satisfied	Neither satisfied nor dissatisfied	Fairly dissatisfied	Very dissatisfied	Don't know or Not applicable	Very important	Fairly important	Neither important nor unimportant	Fairly unimportant	Very unimportant	Don't know or Not applicable
Range of books												
Course books and essential texts												
Range of e-books												
Range of print journals												
Range of electronic journals												
Photocopying												
Printing												
Study facilities (study desks, etc.)												
Provision of PCs												
Reliability of PCs												
Library catalogue												
Library website (other than library catalogue)												
Range of electronic resources (e.g. Web of Knowledge)												
Opening hours												
Library environment (noise, heating, ambience, etc.)												
Helpfulness of the library staff												
Expertise of the library staff												

13. Please indicate how much you agree or disagree with the following statement:

	Strongly agree	Slightly agree	Neither agree nor disagree	Slightly disagree	Strongly disagree	Don't know or Not applicable
Overall, the library provides a good service to me						

14. Any other comments or suggestions?

Note: If you have a specific question to which you'd like a response, please provide your e-mail address.

Submit survey.

Thank you for completing this questionnaire.

The results will be used to make further improvements to our library and information services.

Appendix B
The LibQUAL+™ template as used by the Glasgow University Library

LibQUAL+™ questionnaire is published by kind permission of Glasgow University Library.

Glasgow University Library

Welcome!

We are committed to improving your library services. Better understanding your expectations will help us tailor those services to your needs.

We are conducting this survey to measure library service quality and identify best practices through the Association of Research Libraries' LibQUAL+™ program.

Please answer all items. The survey will take about **10 minutes** to complete. Thank you for your participation!

Information supplied on this form will be processed in the United States. Data protection legislation requires us to make clear that supplying information on the form is entirely voluntary.

Please rate the following statements (1 is lowest, 9 is highest) by indicating:

Minimum – the number that represents the *minimum* level of service that you would find acceptable.

Desired – the number that represents the level of service that you *personally want*.

Perceived – the number that represents the level of service that *you believe* our library currently provides.

For each item, you must EITHER rate the item in all three columns OR identify the item as 'N/A' (not applicable). Selecting 'N/A' will override all other answers for that item.

When it comes to...	My minimum service level is			My desired service level is			Perceived service performance is			
	Low		High	Low		High	Low		High	N/A
1	Library staff who instill confidence in users	1 2 3 4 5 6 7 8 9		1 2 3 4 5 6 7 8 9			1 2 3 4 5 6 7 8 9			N/A
2	Making electronic resources accessible from my home or office	1 2 3 4 5 6 7 8 9		1 2 3 4 5 6 7 8 9			1 2 3 4 5 6 7 8 9			N/A
3	Library space that inspires study and learning	1 2 3 4 5 6 7 8 9		1 2 3 4 5 6 7 8 9			1 2 3 4 5 6 7 8 9			N/A
4	Giving users individual attention	1 2 3 4 5 6 7 8 9		1 2 3 4 5 6 7 8 9			1 2 3 4 5 6 7 8 9			N/A
5	A library website enabling me to locate information on my own	1 2 3 4 5 6 7 8 9		1 2 3 4 5 6 7 8 9			1 2 3 4 5 6 7 8 9			N/A
6	Teaching me how to access, evaluate, and use information	1 2 3 4 5 6 7 8 9		1 2 3 4 5 6 7 8 9			1 2 3 4 5 6 7 8 9			N/A
7	Library staff who are consistently courteous	1 2 3 4 5 6 7 8 9		1 2 3 4 5 6 7 8 9			1 2 3 4 5 6 7 8 9			N/A

When it comes to...	My minimum service level is				My desired service level is				Perceived service performance is			
	Low			High	Low			High	Low			High / N/A
8 The printed library materials I need for my work	1 2 3 4 5 6 7 8 9				1 2 3 4 5 6 7 8 9				1 2 3 4 5 6 7 8 9			N/A
9 Quiet space for individual work	1 2 3 4 5 6 7 8 9				1 2 3 4 5 6 7 8 9				1 2 3 4 5 6 7 8 9			N/A
10 Readiness to respond to users' enquiries	1 2 3 4 5 6 7 8 9				1 2 3 4 5 6 7 8 9				1 2 3 4 5 6 7 8 9			N/A
11 The electronic information resources I need	1 2 3 4 5 6 7 8 9				1 2 3 4 5 6 7 8 9				1 2 3 4 5 6 7 8 9			N/A
12 Access to photocopying and printing facilities	1 2 3 4 5 6 7 8 9				1 2 3 4 5 6 7 8 9				1 2 3 4 5 6 7 8 9			N/A
13 Library staff who have the knowledge to answer user questions	1 2 3 4 5 6 7 8 9				1 2 3 4 5 6 7 8 9				1 2 3 4 5 6 7 8 9			N/A
14 Availability of subject specialist assistance	1 2 3 4 5 6 7 8 9				1 2 3 4 5 6 7 8 9				1 2 3 4 5 6 7 8 9			N/A
15 A comfortable and inviting location	1 2 3 4 5 6 7 8 9				1 2 3 4 5 6 7 8 9				1 2 3 4 5 6 7 8 9			N/A

When it comes to...	My minimum service level is		My desired service level is		Perceived service performance is	
	Low ... High		Low ... High		Low ... High	N/A
16 Library staff who deal with users in a caring fashion	1 2 3 4 5 6 7 8 9		1 2 3 4 5 6 7 8 9		1 2 3 4 5 6 7 8 9	N/A
17 Modern equipment that lets me easily access needed information	1 2 3 4 5 6 7 8 9		1 2 3 4 5 6 7 8 9		1 2 3 4 5 6 7 8 9	N/A
18 Ability to navigate library web pages easily	1 2 3 4 5 6 7 8 9		1 2 3 4 5 6 7 8 9		1 2 3 4 5 6 7 8 9	N/A
19 Library staff who understand the needs of their users	1 2 3 4 5 6 7 8 9		1 2 3 4 5 6 7 8 9		1 2 3 4 5 6 7 8 9	N/A
20 Easy-to-use access tools that allow me to find things on my own	1 2 3 4 5 6 7 8 9		1 2 3 4 5 6 7 8 9		1 2 3 4 5 6 7 8 9	N/A
21 A haven for study, learning, or research	1 2 3 4 5 6 7 8 9		1 2 3 4 5 6 7 8 9		1 2 3 4 5 6 7 8 9	N/A
22 Willingness to help users	1 2 3 4 5 6 7 8 9		1 2 3 4 5 6 7 8 9		1 2 3 4 5 6 7 8 9	N/A

When it comes to...	My minimum service level is			My desired service level is			Perceived service performance is		
	Low		High	Low		High	Low		High / N/A
23 Making information easily accessible for independent use	1 2 3	4 5 6	7 8 9	1 2 3	4 5 6	7 8 9	1 2 3	4 5 6	7 8 9 N/A
24 Print and/or electronic journal collections I require for my work	1 2 3	4 5 6	7 8 9	1 2 3	4 5 6	7 8 9	1 2 3	4 5 6	7 8 9 N/A
25 Space for group learning and group study	1 2 3	4 5 6	7 8 9	1 2 3	4 5 6	7 8 9	1 2 3	4 5 6	7 8 9 N/A
26 Timely document delivery/interlibrary loan	1 2 3	4 5 6	7 8 9	1 2 3	4 5 6	7 8 9	1 2 3	4 5 6	7 8 9 N/A
27 Dependability in handling users' service problems	1 2 3	4 5 6	7 8 9	1 2 3	4 5 6	7 8 9	1 2 3	4 5 6	7 8 9 N/A

	Please indicate the degree to which you agree with the following statements:	
28	The library helps me stay abreast of developments in my field(s) of interest.	1 2 3 4 5 6 7 8 9 *Strongly Disagree* *Strongly Agree*
29	The library aids my advancement in my academic discipline.	1 2 3 4 5 6 7 8 9 *Strongly Disagree* *Strongly Agree*
30	The library enables me to be more efficient in my academic pursuits.	1 2 3 4 5 6 7 8 9 *Strongly Disagree* *Strongly Agree*
31	The library helps me distinguish between trustworthy and untrustworthy information.	1 2 3 4 5 6 7 8 9 *Strongly Disagree* *Strongly Agree*
32	The library provides me with the information skills I need in my work or study.	1 2 3 4 5 6 7 8 9 *Strongly Disagree* *Strongly Agree*
33	In general, I am satisfied with the way in which I am treated at the library.	1 2 3 4 5 6 7 8 9 *Strongly Disagree* *Strongly Agree*
34	In general, I am satisfied with library support for my learning, research, and/or teaching needs.	1 2 3 4 5 6 7 8 9 *Strongly Disagree* *Strongly Agree*
35	How would you rate the overall quality of the service provided by the library?	1 2 3 4 5 6 7 8 9 *Extremely Poor* *Extremely Good*

	Please indicate your library usage patterns:	
36	How often do you use resources within the library?	– Daily – Weekly – Monthly – Quarterly – Never
37	How often do you access library resources through a library web page?	– Daily – Weekly – Monthly – Quarterly – Never
38	How often do you use Yahoo(TM), Google(TM), or non-library gateways for information?	– Daily – Weekly – Monthly – Quarterly – Never

	Please answer a few questions about yourself:	
39	The library that you use most often:	– Main Library – Adam Smith Library – Chemistry Branch Library – James Herriot Library – James Ireland Memorial Library – Reading Room
40	Age:	– Under 18 – 18–22 – 23–30 – 31–45 – 46–65 – Over 65
41	Sex:	– Male – Female
42	Full or part-time student?	– Full-time – Part-time – Does not apply/NA

43. Discipline:

- Accountancy & Finance
- Arts & Humanities
- Biomedical & Life Sciences
- Business & Management Studies
- Computing Sciences
- Dentistry
- Divinity
- Education
- Engineering
- Information & Mathematical Sciences
- Law & Financial Studies
- Medicine
- Nursing Studies
- Physical Sciences
- Psychology

- Science Undergraduate
- Social Sciences
- Sports Sciences
- Statistics
- Veterinary Medicine

44. Position:

(Select the ONE option that best describes you.)

Undergraduate:
- First year
- Second year
- Third year
- Fourth year
- Fifth year and above
- Non-degree

Postgraduate:
- Taught Masters degree
- Research Masters degree
- Doctoral Research degree
- Non-degree
- Undecided

Academic staff:
- Professor
- Reader
- Senior/Principal Lecturer
- Lecturer
- Research Staff
- Other Academic Status

Library staff:
- – Senior Management
- – Department Head/Team Leader
- – Professional Staff
- – Support Staff
- – Other

Staff:
- – Administrative or Academic Related Staff
- – Other staff positions

45. **Please enter any comments about library services in the box below:**

_____
_____
_____
_____
_____
_____
_____
_____
_____
_____

46. **Enter your e-mail address in the box below if you would like to enter an optional drawing for a prize. Your e-mail address will be kept confidential and will not be linked to your survey responses. (Not required)**

_____

Thank you for participating in this library service quality survey!

Appendix C
The PLUS questionnaire for adults

The PLUS questionnaires are published by kind permission of the Institute of Public Finance Ltd.

This is a national survey to find out how well your library service meets your needs. At the end of your visit, please complete this questionnaire and place it in the box. Staff will be happy to help. Thank you.

Section A

What did you do on your visit to the library today?

Please tick ✓ all that apply

Borrow/return/renew book(s)	☐
Borrow/return/renew cassette(s)	☐
Borrow/return/renew CD(s)	☐
Borrow/return/renew video(s)	☐
Borrow/return/renew DVD(s)	☐
Borrow/return/renew CD-ROM(s)	☐
Browse	☐
Seek information/find something out	☐

Read newspaper(s)/magazine(s) ☐

Attend an event/exhibition ☐

Use a computer ☐

Use the Internet ☐

Sit to study/work/read book(s) ☐

Use a photocopier ☐

Something else, please tell us: ☐

Section B

Please tell us about what you were looking for today

1. How many items (books, cassettes, CDs, videos, DVDs etc.) are you taking away with you today?

    ☐ ☐

    example: 0 2

2a. If you were looking for one or more specific books to take home with you today, please write them down and tell us if you found them or not:

    example: **Yes** **No**

    Dr Jekyll and Mr Hyde ✓

	Yes	**No**
	☐	☐
	☐	☐
	☐	☐

2b. If you came to the library today without a particular book in mind, did you find any to borrow?

    Yes **No**

    ☐ ☐

3a. If you were looking for one or more specific cassettes, CDs, videos or DVDs to take home with you today, please write them down and tell us if you found them or not:

	Yes	No
example:		
Laurel and Hardy		✓

	Yes	No
_____	☐	☐
_____	☐	☐
_____	☐	☐

3b. If you came to the library today without a particular cassette/CD/video/DVD in mind, did you find any to borrow?

	Yes	No
	☐	☐

4. Information and enquiries:
If you came to find something out, were you successful in finding it?

Yes	In part	No
☐	☐	☐

Section C

Please tell us what you think of *this* library

All library users:

Please tick ✓ one per line	Very Good	Good	Adequate	Poor	Very Poor
Condition of the library outside	☐	☐	☐	☐	☐
Condition of the library inside	☐	☐	☐	☐	☐
Ease of access entering the library	☐	☐	☐	☐	☐

Ease of access inside the library	☐	☐	☐	☐	☐
Signs and guiding	☐	☐	☐	☐	☐
Layout and arrangement	☐	☐	☐	☐	☐
Provision of seating and tables	☐	☐	☐	☐	☐
Hours of opening	☐	☐	☐	☐	☐
Books and other materials	☐	☐	☐	☐	☐
Time spent waiting for service	☐	☐	☐	☐	☐
Staff helpfulness	☐	☐	☐	☐	☐
Staff knowledge and expertise	☐	☐	☐	☐	☐
Information and enquiry services	☐	☐	☐	☐	☐
Children's services	☐	☐	☐	☐	☐
Computers	☐	☐	☐	☐	☐
Overall	☐	☐	☐	☐	☐

Mobile library users only:

Time of day the library calls in my area	☐	☐	☐	☐	☐
Frequency with which the library visits my area	☐	☐	☐	☐	☐
Convenience of stopping location in my area	☐	☐	☐	☐	☐
Punctuality of visits	☐	☐	☐	☐	☐

Section D

Please tell us about yourself

The following questions are optional. The information given below will only be used by the library in connection with its services.

1. How often do you usually visit this library?

Please tick ✓ one

This is my first visit (to this library)	☐
More than once a week`	☐
About once a week	☐
About once a fortnight	☐
About once every three weeks	☐
About once every four weeks	☐
Less frequently (than four weeks)	☐

2. Age group:

Please tick ✓ one

14 or under	☐
15–19	☐
20–24	☐
25–34	☐
35–44	☐
45–54	☐
55–64	☐
65–74	☐
75 or over	☐

3. Gender:

Please tick ✓ one

Female ☐

Male ☐

4. Your postcode:

e.g. M K 4 2   9 W A

5. Are you:

Please tick ✓ all that apply

In full-time employment ☐

In part-time employment ☐

Self-employed ☐

Unemployed ☐

Retired ☐

A part-time student ☐

A full-time student ☐

Looking after the home/family ☐

Permanently sick/disabled ☐

Other, please say what: ☐

Please continue on supplemental sheet

Appendix D
The PLUS questionnaire for children

The PLUS questionnaires are published by kind permission of the Institute of Public Finance Ltd.

If you need large print, braille or a taped version please ask a member of staff. Please do not write your name on this form.

1. **What I am**

   please mark ☒ in one box

   ☐ I am a boy

   ☐ I am a girl

2. **What was your age on your last birthday?**

	years

   example | 9 | years

   please mark ☒ here ☐ if aged under 1

3. **My postcode is**

   example   M   K   4   2   9   W   A

If you don't know your postcode please write down your home address:

```



```

4. How often I visit this library

please mark ☒ in one box

☐ This is my first time here

☐ I come here more than once a week

☐ I come here once a week

☐ I come here less than once a week

5. Who I came with

please mark ☒ in as many boxes as you like

☐ Today I came here with my mum or dad

☐ Today I came here with my brother or sister

☐ Today I came here with friends

☐ Today I came here on my own

☐ Today I came here with someone else, please say who:

```


```

6. I have my own library card for this library

please mark ☒ in one box

☐ Yes

☐ No

7. What I will do in the library today

please mark ☒ in as many boxes as you like

☐ I came to join the library

☐ I came to borrow a book

☐ I came to find something out

☐ I came to borrow music CDs

☐ I came to borrow story tapes or CDs

☐ I came to borrow videos or DVDs

☐ I came to return something

☐ I came to read

☐ I came to do my homework

☐ I came to use the Internet or computer

☐ I came for a storytime or event

☐ I came to look around

☐ I came to meet friends

☐ I came to play

☐ I came for somewhere to go

☐ I came for something else, please say what:

8. What I think of this library

please mark ☒ in only one box on each line

	Good	OK	Bad
I think the books are	☐	☐	☐
I think the music CDs are	☐	☐	☐
I think the story tapes or CDs are	☐	☐	☐
I think the videos or DVDs are	☐	☐	☐
I think the computers are	☐	☐	☐

I think the information to help
with my homework is   ☐   ☐   ☐

I think the space for me to sit and
work is   ☐   ☐   ☐

I think the storytimes or events are   ☐   ☐   ☐

I think the library looks   ☐   ☐   ☐

I think the library opening times are   ☐   ☐   ☐

I think the library staff are   ☐   ☐   ☐

I think the help I get from the
library staff with my homework is   ☐   ☐   ☐

I think the help I get from the
library staff choosing books is   ☐   ☐   ☐

Overall I think this library is   ☐   ☐   ☐

9. **I found something out in the library today**
   please mark ☒ in one box

   ☐ Yes

   ☐ No

10. **I used the Internet or computers in the library today**
    please mark ☒ in one box

    ☐ Yes

    ☐ No

11. **At the end of my visit today I took books home**
    please mark ☒ in one box

    ☐ Yes

    ☐ No

12. At the end of my visit today I took cassettes, CDs, DVDs or videos home

please mark ☒ in one box

☐ Yes

☐ No

Please write down any ideas you have that would make the library better for you

---

Thank you for your help

Bibliography

Andretta, S. (2005) *Information Literacy: A Practitioners' Guide*. Oxford: Chandos Publishing.

Armstrong, C. (2001) 'Low ICT use by students', *Library Association Record* 103(6): 358–9.

Baruchson-Arbib, S. and Shor, F. (2002) 'Perspectives on the use of electronic information sources by Israeli college students', *Journal of Academic Librarianship* 28(4): 255–7.

Bertot, J. C. (2004) 'Libraries and networked information services: issues and consideration in measurement'. In 5th Northumbria International Conference on Performance Measurement in Libraries and Information Services. Parker, S. (ed.) *Library Measures to Fill the Void: Assessing the Outcomes*. Bradford: Emerald; pp. 3–11.

Black, A. and Crann, M. (2002) 'In the public eye: a mass observation of the public library'. *Journal of Librarianship and Information Science* 34(3): 145–57.

Blagden, J. and Harrington, J. (1990) *How Good is Your Library? A Review of Approaches to the Evaluation of Library & Information Services*. London: Aslib.

Blagden, P. (2005) 'The LIRG/SCONUL Measuring Impact Initiative: overview of phase 1 impact projects', *Library & Information Research* 29(91): 20–2.

Book Marketing Limited (2003) *Student Information Sources and Book Buying Behaviour 2003*. London: Book Marketing Limited.

Booth, A. and Brice, A. (2004) *Evidence Based Practice for Information Professionals: A Handbook*. London: Facet Publishing.

Boylan, H. R. (2004) 'Issues of student performance, retention and institutional change', In Osborne, M., Gallacher, J. and Crossan, B. (eds) *Researching Widening Access to Lifelong Learning: Issues and Approaches in International Research*. London: Routledge Falmer; pp. 103–14.

Brennan, J. and Williams, R. (2004) *Collecting and Using Student Feedback: A Guide to Good Practice*. York: Learning and Teaching Support Network.

Brice, A. and Booth, A. (2004) 'Consider the evidence'. *Library and Information Update* 3(6): 32–3.

British Standards Institution (1998) *Information and Documentation: Library Performance Indicators*. London: BSI (International Standard ISO 11620).

Brockman, J. (ed.) (1997) *Quality Management and Benchmarking in the Information Sector*. London: Bowker Saur.

Brophy, P. (2002) *The Evaluation of Public Library Online Services: Measuring Impact. The People's Network*. Workshop Series Issue Papers no. 1.

Buzdygan, D., Różycka, M., Sobielga, J. and Tomczak E. (2000) 'Badanie potrzeb użytkowników'. *EBIB: Materialy konferencyjne* 1. Available at: *http://ebib.oss .wroc.pl/matkonf/atr/buzdygan.html* (last accessed: 6 January 2006).

Coates, T. (2004) *Who's in Charge?: Responsibility for the Public Library Service*. Available at: *http://www.libri .org.uk/*.

Cook, C., Heath F. and Thompson, B. (2004) 'LibQUAL +™ from the UK perspective'. In 5th Northumbria

International Conference on Performance Measurement in Libraries and Information Services. Parker, S. (ed.) *Library Measures to Fill the Void: Assessing the Outcomes*. Bradford: Emerald; pp. 156–9.

Corrall, S. (2002) 'Planning and policy making'. In Melling M. and Little, J. (eds) *Building a Successful Customer-Service Culture: A Guide For Library And Information Managers*. London: Facet; pp. 27–52.

Craven, J. and Brophy, P. (2004) 'Evaluating the longitudinal impact of networked services in UK public libraries: the Longitude 2 project'. In 5th Northumbria International Conference on Performance Measurement in Libraries and Information Services. Parker, S. (ed.) *Library Measures to Fill the Void: Assessing the Outcomes*. Bradford: Emerald; pp. 223–7.

Crawford, J. (2000) *Evaluation of Library and Information Services*. 2nd edn. London: Aslib.

Crawford, J. (2006) 'The use of electronic information services and information literacy: a Glasgow Caledonian University study', *Journal of Librarianship and Information Science* 38(1): 33–44.

Crawford, J., De Vicente, A. and Clink S. (2004) 'Use and awareness of electronic information services by students at Glasgow Caledonian University: a longitudinal study', *Journal of Librarianship and Information Science* 36(3): 101–17.

Crawford, J. C. (1999) 'A qualitative study of the use of networked software and electronic information services at Glasgow Caledonian University Library', *Education for Information* 17(2): 101–11.

Crawford, J. C. and Daye, A. (2000) 'A survey of the use of electronic services at Glasgow Caledonian University Library', *The Electronic Library* 18(4): 255–65.

Creaser, C. (2001) 'Performance measurement and benchmarking for schools library services', *Journal of Librarianship and Information Science* 33(3): 126–32.

Creaser, C. (2004). 'Measuring and comparing: statistical benchmarking for academic libraries'. In 5th Northumbria International Conference on Performance Measurement in Libraries and Information Services. Parker, S. (ed.) *Library Measures to Fill the Void: Assessing the Outcomes*. Bradford: Emerald; pp. 58–63.

Creaser, C. (2005) 'Benchmarking the standard SCONUL user survey: report of a pilot study', *SCONUL Focus* 34 (Spring): pp. 61–5.

Davies, E. and Creaser, C. (2005) 'Taking a measured approach to library management: performance evidence applications and culture', paper presented at IFLA Marketing & Management Section Satellite Meeting, Bergen, 9–11th August. 71st IFLA General Conference and Council: 14th–18th August, Oslo.

Department for Education and Skills and Department for Work and Pensions (2005). *Skills, Getting on in Business, Getting on at Work*. 3 vols. London: Department for Education and Skills.

Gannon-Leary, P., Banwell, L. and Parker, S. (2003) 'An evaluation of the development of the People's Network in the North East', *Library & Information Research* 27(87): 5–16.

Gorman, G. E. and Clayton, P. (2005) *Qualitative Research For The Information Professional: A Practical Handbook* 2nd edn. London: Facet.

Groombridge, B. (1964) *The Londoner and His Library*. London: Research Institute for Consumer Affairs.

Hart, L. (2002) 'Benchmarking for improvement'. In Creaser, C. (ed.) *Statistics in Practice: Measuring & Managing: Proceedings of IFLA Satellite Conference,*

Loughborough, August, 2002. Loughborough: Library & Information Statistics Unit. LISU Occasional Paper no 32. pp. 30–9.

Hernon, P. and Altman, E. (1998) *Assessing Service Quality: Satisfying the Expectations of Library Customers.* Chicago and London: American Library Association.

Hernon, P. and Whitman, J. R. (2001) *Delivering Satisfaction and Service Quality.* Chicago: American Library Association.

Hewitson, A. (2002) 'EIS student survey' unpublished internal report, Leeds Metropolitan University.

Higher Education Funding Council for England. *Information on Quality and Standards in Higher Education: Final Report of the Task Group* (Cooke report) (2002) Bristol, HEFCE.

Hull, B. (2001) 'Barriers to libraries as agents of lifelong learning'. *Library and Information Briefings* 105 (July): 1–12.

Jubilee (2004) *JISC User Behaviour in Information Seeking: Longitudinal Evaluation of Electronic Information services. Fifth annual report, final report, August.* Newcastle: Northumbria University.

King Research Ltd. (1990) *Keys to Success: Performance Indicators for Public Libraries.* (Library Information series no. 18). London: Office of Arts and Libraries.

Kyrillidou, M. and Heath, F. M. (2001) 'Introduction [to Measuring service quality]', *Library Trends* 49(4): 541–7.

Laser Foundation (2005) *Libraries Impact Project.* PricewaterhouseCoopers LLP, July. Available at: *http://www.bl.uk/about/cooperation/pdf/laserfinal6.pdf* (last accessed: 6 January 2006).

Macnaught, B. (2004) 'Impact and performance measurement in public library services in the UK'. In 5th Northumbria International Conference on Performance

Measurement in Libraries and Information Services. Parker S. (ed.) *Library Measures to Fill the Void: Assessing the Outcomes.* Bradford: Emerald; pp. 18–22.

McNicol, S. (2004a) 'Investigating non-use of libraries in the UK using the mass-observation archive'. *Journal of Librarianship and Information Science* 36(2): 79–87.

McNicol, S. (2004b) 'Is research an untapped resource in the library and information profession?' *Journal of Librarianship and Information Science* 36(3): 119–26.

MORI Social Research Institute (2005) *Understanding the Audience.* Available at: *http://www.common-info.org.uk/mori-findings.shtml.*

Muddiman, D., Durrani, S., Dutch, M., Linley, R., Pateman, J. and Vincent, J. (2000) *Open to All? The Public Library and Social Exclusion. Vol. 1: Overview and Conclusions.* London: Resource.

Mundt, S. (2003) 'Benchmarking user satisfaction in academic libraries: a case study', *Library & Information Research* 27(87): 29–37.

Nowacka, J. (2002) 'An analysis of local community needs as the basis for library services offered by the public library in Suwalki'. *EBIB 2.* Available at: *http://ebib.oss .wroc.pl/english/grant/nowacka.php* (last accessed: 6 January 2006).

Obst, O. (1995) 'Untersuchung der Internetbenutzung durch Bibliothekskunden an der Universitaets- and Landesbibliothek (ULB) Muenster', *Bibliotheksdienst,* 29(12): 1980–98.

Pateman, J. (2004) 'Developing a needs-based service'. *Library and Information Update* 3(5): 34–7.

Payne, P. and Conyers, A. (2005) 'Measuring the impact of higher education libraries: The LIRG/SCONUL Impact Implementation Initiative', *Library & Information Research* 29(91): 3–9.

Poll, R. and te Boekhorst, P. (1996) *Measuring Quality: International Guidelines for Performance Measurement in Academic Libraries*. Muenchen: Saur.

Revill, D. and Ford, G. (1996) *User Satisfaction: Standard Survey Forms for Academic Libraries*. London: SCONUL (SCONUL Briefing Paper).

Savage, E. A. (1937) 'The distribution of book borrowing in Edinburgh'. *Library Association Record*, April: 150–6.

Seamans, N. H. (2002) 'Student perceptions of information literacy: insights for librarians', *Reference Services Review* (30)2: 112–23.

Seidler-de Alwis, R. and Fuehles-Ubach, S. (2004) 'Importance of measuring in-library usage', *Library and Information Update* 3(9): 40–1.

Self, J. (2004) 'Metrics and management: applying the results of the balanced scorecard'. In 5th Northumbria International Conference on Performance Measurement in Libraries and Information Services. Parker, S. (ed.) *Library Measures to Fill the Void: Assessing the Outcomes*. Bradford: Emerald; pp. 135–9.

Stephen, P. and Hornby, S. (1997) *Simple Statistics for Library and Information Professionals*. 2nd edn. London: Library Association Publishing.

Sumsion, J. (2002) 'ISO 2789: what's new in and around revision?', *Performance Measurement and Metrics* 3(1): 10–19.

Town, S. (2004a) 'Filling the void or bridging the deep? LibQUAL+™ in the UK'. In 5th Northumbria International Conference on Performance Measurement in Libraries and Information Services. Parker, S. (ed.) *Library Measures to Fill the Void: Assessing the Outcomes*. Bradford: Emerald; pp. 212–19.

Town, S. (2004b) 'E-measures: a comprehensive waste of time?' *Vine* 34(4): 190–5.

University of Oxford (1931) *Library Provision in Oxford: Report and Recommendations of the Commission Appointed by the Congregation of the University.* Oxford: Oxford University Press.

Van House, N., Weil, B.T. and McClure, C. R. (1990) *Measuring Academic Library Performance: A Practical Approach.* Chicago: American Library Association.

Waldman, M. (2003) 'Freshmen's use of library electronic resources and self-efficacy', *Information Research* 8(2): 1–24.

Walters, W. H. (2003) 'Expertise and evidence in the assessment of library service quality' *Performance Measurement and Metrics* 4(3): 98–102.

West, C. (2001) *Measuring User Satisfaction: A Practical Guide for Academic Libraries.* London: SCONUL; pp. 2–13.

West, C. (2004) 'A survey of surveys'. *SCONUL Newsletter* 31 (Spring): 18–22.

Williams, D. and Wavell, C. (2001) *The Impact of the School Library Resource Centre on Learning. Library and Information Commission Research Report 112.* Aberdeen: Robert Gordon University for Resource.

Wynne, P. M and Clarke, Z. (2000) 'Towards an inclusive methodology for the measurement of inhouse use'. *Journal of Librarianship and Information Science* 32(2): 82–90.

Index

Printed in the United Kingdom
by Lightning Source UK Ltd.
108934UKS00002B/25-69